Teachi

Teaching Spelling: Exploring commonsense strategies and best practices equips teachers with the vital knowledge and skills needed to help their students become proficient writers and spellers.

Peter Westwood provides a very clear and concise account of the important skills and processes that underpin accurate spelling, and he describes in very practical terms, many evidence-based strategies and methods that teachers can use to help all students become confident, capable and independent spellers. The book also addresses the purposes of various forms of assessment of spelling skills, to guide teaching and planning.

Chapters in this accessible and timely text include:

- the importance of correct spelling
- visual, auditory and cognitive components of spelling ability
- general principles for planning instruction
- proven teaching strategies and methods
- word study as a teaching approach
- formal and informal assessment.

At the end of each chapter the author provides a list of online and print resources, thus enabling readers to extend their knowledge in the various topics. The extensive reference list is also an invaluable source of information on recent research and thinking on the topic of spelling instruction.

Teaching Spelling is an essential resource for all those in teacher education and taking in-service courses.

Peter Westwood has taught in schools and universities for many years and is currently an editor and freelance education writer. His most recently published books with Routledge include *Commonsense Methods for Children with Special Educational Needs*, 2011, now in its sixth edition, and *Inclusive and Adaptive Teaching*, 2013.

Teaching Spelling

Exploring commonsense strategies and best practices

Peter Westwood

Routledge
Taylor & Francis Group

LONDON AND NEW YORK

First published 2014
by Routledge
2 Park Square, Milton Park, Abingdon, Oxon OX14 4RN

and by Routledge
711 Third Avenue, New York, NY 10017

Routledge is an imprint of the Taylor & Francis Group, an informa business

© 2014 P. Westwood

British Library Cataloguing in Publication Data
A catalogue record for this book is available from the British Library

Library of Congress Cataloging in Publication Data
Westwood, Peter S.
Teaching spelling : exploring commonsense strategies and best practices / Peter Westwood.
pages cm
English language--Orthography and spelling--Study and teaching. I. Title.
LB1574.W47 2014
372.63'2--dc23
2013035117

ISBN: 978-0-415-73993-1 (hbk)
ISBN: 978-0-415-73994-8 (pbk)
ISBN: 978-1-315-81590-9 (ebk)

Typeset in Sabon and Gill
by Saxon Graphics Ltd, Derby

Printed and bound by CPI Group (UK) Ltd, Croydon, CR0 4YY

Contents

Introduction

The renewed emphasis on teaching spelling in primary and secondary schools can be traced back to concerns expressed online and in the community that students' standard of spelling seems to have declined over the past three decades. Rightly or wrongly, it is felt by many parents in recent years that schools were doing too little to teach their children how to spell. This situation was linked partly to the now discredited 'whole-language' approach to literacy. Under that approach, students were expected to learn to spell merely by engaging in daily writing and being exposed to print. Formal instruction in spelling and phonics became unfashionable.

Surveys in Britain and Australia added to the perception of poor spelling standards. It was found from test results that too many students in both countries were failing to achieve minimum standards in spelling. It was even reported that the accuracy of spelling of some teachers left much to be desired (Taylor, 2004; TESS, 2005). In the US similar concerns were voiced concerning both students and teachers.

In response to these concerns, revisions to the National Curriculum in Britain now include clearly stated standards for spelling at various age levels; and students' spelling ability is formally tested at Key Stage 2. Similarly, the new Australian Curriculum has given due importance to the teaching and testing of spelling in both primary and secondary schools. Under guidelines provided for the Australian Curriculum, spelling is to be taught as an integral part of the broader study of language, and is formally tested at school in Years 3, 5, 7 and 9. In the US, in November 2012, the powerful National Council of Teachers of English and the International Reading Association (IRA) reaffirmed the Standards for English Language Arts (NCTE, 2012). These standards include specific reference to students needing to master language conventions (spelling and punctuation). And in each state in the US published standards now contain much more detail of what students are expected to achieve in spelling at various grade levels (e.g., MDE, 2010; OSPI Washington, 2010).

The aim of this book is to provide teachers and parents with information that is relevant to improving spelling standards, and also for assisting those students who continue to struggle to achieve adequate proficiency. The first four chapters provide important background information on the knowledge, skills and processes that underpin proficiency in spelling. The remaining five chapters describe research-based approaches to teaching and assessment.

Additional resources for teachers are listed at the end of each chapter; and the Appendix contains a number of items useful for teaching specific principles embodied in English spelling. Some of this material can also be used selectively for assessing students' current word knowledge and spelling skills.

It is reassuring to find that education policy-makers in Britain, Australia and the US are now promoting the more effective teaching of spelling skills to students of all ages. It now remains for this good intention to be translated into best practice in our classrooms.

Peter Westwood

Chapter 1

Is accurate spelling still important?

Once upon a time, many years ago, society valued accurate spelling in all forms of written communication. It is only in more recent years, with the advent of electronic text messaging by the masses, that correct spelling has been abandoned by some in favour of cute abbreviations, invented terms, and shorthand contractions of everyday words—all commonly referred now to as 'textisms' (Wood *et al.*, 2011). This situation has prompted Reed (2012, p.1) to pose a pertinent question. She asks:

> Has spelling become an antiquated concept in this world of instantaneous online referencing, automatic document spellchecking, and the public's disheartening patience with a poorly spelled word? In every teacher's crowded instruction schedule, does spelling have a place—or has it become an anachronism, its instructional power fading with the intense focus and scrutiny on other literacy skills considered to be more critical?

Reed then goes on to justify in detail why teaching students to spell is indeed still vitally important; and she suggests that research-based approaches are the most effective. This view is fully supported by Jones (2009) and Leipzig (2000) who recommend teaching spelling as an essential aspect of learning about language. Teaching spelling also fully supports underlying knowledge and skills required in reading and vocabulary development.

Current standards in spelling

Perhaps it is a sign of the times that The English Spelling Society (TESS, 2005) has cited sources that indicate poor spelling standards among university students. They also refer to classroom teachers who regularly make spelling mistakes on school reports. This is not entirely surprising, as many of our teachers went to school as students during the period 1970 to 1990, when the teaching of spelling was neglected. And when they later trained as teachers, their colleges and universities devoted little or no time to pedagogy related to such basic skills instruction (Manning and Tibshraeny, 2013).

Newspaper and other media reports frequently express concern about falling standards of spelling in our schools—and this includes teachers' own spelling (e.g., Alphonso, 2013; Bradford, 2012; Morris, 2013). Perhaps Debbie Hepplewhite (2008, p.2) is right to ask: 'Has everyone given up on spelling?'

Do our schools still teach spelling?

The importance placed by schools on the teaching of spelling has varied over the years. Traditionally—until the mid-1970s—primary schools almost always devoted specific time and attention to teaching and testing of spelling within the weekly classroom programme. This tradition most often involved the children memorizing a weekly spelling list containing words appropriate for their grade level, plus a few new words that had been introduced within specific subject areas of the curriculum. Teachers were also diligent in their marking of spelling errors that occurred in children's written work, and these errors then had to be corrected by the children through repetitive practice. This approach was at least systematic; and most children (but certainly not all) did learn to spell to an acceptable standard.

What was missing from most classrooms at that time was any direct teaching of *cognitive strategies* that can help children learn, remember and check words more effectively (Berninger *et al.*, 2013; Morris and Smith, 2011, Watson, 2013). Under the traditional approach, children resorted to rote learning without appreciating that there were other, more effective, ways to master the spelling of English words. As Joshi *et al.* (2009) have pointed out, spelling should be a *thinking process*, and should not be a matter of rote memorization. They go on to state:

> Students should be taught about the lawfulness of spelling, even while irregularities are acknowledged. Students can be encouraged to recognize, learn, and use the patterns in English spelling through systematic, explicit instruction and activities. Such instruction requires careful planning, but is much more effective than memorizing words in a rote fashion.
>
> (Joshi *et al.*, 2009, p.12)

By the 1970s, the literacy 'experts' of the time in the US, Australia, New Zealand and Britain began to question the effectiveness of what they regarded as an approach to spelling that ignored context. They suggested that spelling should never be taught as a separate topic, arguing instead that children learn to spell most easily and naturally as they engage in the act of writing to communicate their ideas. Individual help would be provided for them at the most 'teachable moment' during the lesson, just when they needed to spell an unfamiliar word. They also argued that it was pointless to try to teach spelling, particularly using knowledge of letter-to-sound correspondences, because English is just too unpredictable. These beliefs became firmly embedded as key tenets within what became known as the 'whole-language' and 'real writing' approach—influencing the teaching of literacy skills for the next 20 years. The net result was that teachers in early primary classes eventually devoted almost no time at all to teaching spelling principles (Cooke, Slee and Young, 2008).

Renewed emphasis on spelling

Now that the whole-language approach for reading and writing has largely been discredited as a complete method for developing literacy (Dehaene, 2009; Gentry, 2010), we must ask if the pendulum has swung back in favour of teaching spelling skills explicitly. The signs are that it has. Along with an increased emphasis on the direct teaching of phonic skills in early reading, there has been a welcome return to teaching children to spell (e.g., Alderman and Green, 2011; DfE [UK], 2012a; Puranik and Alotaiba, 2012; Werfel and Schuele, 2012). In the revised version of the National Curriculum in the UK for example, there is an increased focus now on spelling, with clear indications of what all children should be able to achieve in spelling by the end of primary school years (DfE [UK], 2012a). Spelling ability, alongside grammar and punctuation will be formally assessed in all schools at the end of Key Stage 2. Similarly, in the new Australian Curriculum spelling is seen now as an important focus in both primary *and secondary* schools, and the required knowledge, skills and standards at each year level are now set out explicitly (ACARA, 2011a; 2011b; 2012). The current situation in both countries is reflected accurately by Massey and Dexter (2002, p.3) when they state: 'A political consensus now recognizes that accurate writing is a basic requirement for life outside school, especially in employment, and that inaccurate written work should be unacceptable in schools.' More is said in Chapter 9 about the role of testing spelling within national curricula.

In the US, there is also evidence that most elementary school teachers may have moved beyond the previous whole-language 'incidental' learning approach. In 2003, a national study in the US found that 98 per cent of respondents reported that they now spend specific teaching time each week on spelling; and 73 per cent firmly believe that students need formal spelling instruction (Fresch, 2003). Commenting on this change, Matchan (2012, p.1) has observed: 'Spelling, which suffered a precipitous drop in status during the last few years, has become popular again.' However, Gentry (2010) warns that too many US elementary schools still make excuses for not providing 15 minutes a day of direct and systematic instruction in spelling. And more than 60 per cent of the teachers surveyed by Fresch (2003) still relied almost entirely on published basal spelling programmes for their curriculum content, and were not overly confident in how best to *teach* spelling strategies. A common weakness of published programmes is that often they are not based on a sound underlying theory of how words should be studied, stored and remembered (Davis, 2011).

The beginnings of the renewed interest in teaching spelling in the US can be traced back to the 1990s, when several American educators produced materials that encouraged a more systematic approach to phonics and word study (e.g., Bear, Invernizzi and Johnson, 1995; Cunningham, 1995; Ganske, 2000; Zutell, 1998). In support of spelling and word study, Templeton (2000) suggested that most students need to examine words carefully apart from simply meeting them in the natural contexts in which they are used in reading and writing. This examination process must involve learners in comparing and contrasting words in an active search for patterns. Such an approach is valuable for all children—but it is deemed absolutely essential for those who are struggling to learn to spell (Brooks, 2007). Word study is discussed fully in Chapter 7.

English spelling is not entirely unpredictable

Despite the claims of many progressive literacy educators, the spelling of English words is not arbitrary and random. Only some 4 per cent of English words are truly irregular, and must be learned visually and by repeated writing. It has been found that nearly 50 per cent of our words are predictable, based on sound-to-letter correspondences, and another 34 per cent are predictable except for one sound (Joshi *et al.*, 2009; Moats, 2005; Templeton and Morris, 2001). This indicates that applying phonic knowledge as a strategy for spelling will be reasonably effective for more than 80 per cent of words—if the target word is being heard clearly and pronounced accurately by the speller.

No word is entirely irregular, and attending to the sounds within a word can give a sufficient clue that allows for an approximate first spelling. Jackson (2008) points out that many words with multiple syllables are actually easier to spell phonetically than some one-syllable words. In addition, when a student begins to recognize and use commonly occurring *groups* of letters (*mental orthographic images*: Wasowicz, 2010) that represent key parts of words (e.g., *pre–, –ight, pho–, –tial, –ay–, str–, –ally*) rather than relying on single-letter encoding, even more English words become easier to spell. However, this does not mean that spelling in English then becomes trouble free—far from it, particularly for some learners.

The strong connection between phonics and spelling is very clear in written languages such as Italian and Finnish, where there is almost entirely regular correspondence between letters and sounds (Davis, 1999; Dehaene, 2009; Upward and Pulcini, 1994). Such languages are said to have 'shallow orthographic depth', and can be contrasted with 'deep' languages where grapheme-phoneme correspondences are much less predictable (Carrillo, Alegria and Marin, 2013). Learning to read and spell in shallow orthographic languages is much easier and quicker (Galletly and Knight, 2013). For historical reasons, contemporary English is regarded as a language with a deep orthography because it contains many words that have been imported from, or influenced by, other languages. Certain words do not obey phonic principles for a variety of purely idiosyncratic reasons, such as errors or inventions made by the early scribes, printers and typesetters. Extremely interesting accounts of the many influences on language and spelling over the years can be found in the writings of David Crystal (e.g., 2005; 2011; 2012). For example, looking back at the written English language in the 1400s he points out:

> There was huge variation in the way words were spelled. A word like *might* appears in manuscripts in over thirty different spellings—*micht, mycht, myght, mihte* and so on. Caxton had to make a choice. Which one was most likely to be most widely understood?
>
> (Crystal, 2011, p.78)

The following three chapters discuss the perceptual and cognitive processes that underpin spelling ability. Knowledge of these processes equips teachers with a better understanding of the purposes of specific teaching approaches, and the reason for assessing students' underlying skills if they have difficulty becoming proficient spellers.

Best practices

- Accurate spelling is still very important. The teaching of spelling should no longer be placed on the back burner and virtually ignored.
- The evidence is that spelling skills need to be explicitly taught, beginning in the kindergarten with a focus on developing phonological skills, and extending on

through the primary and secondary years to include word study in its various forms.

- Best practice is reflected in teaching approaches that stress the logic and rationality behind the spelling of most English words, not in approaches that imply spelling patterns are entirely random and must therefore be memorized by rote.
- The teaching of spelling should be part of a much broader study of the English language, in both oral and written forms.

Online and print resources

- Crystal, D. (2012). *Spell it out: The singular story of English spelling*. London: Profile Books.
- Reed, D.K. (2012). *Why teach spelling?* Portsmouth, NH: Center on Instruction/ RMC Research Corporation. Accessed online 11 October 2012 at: http://www. centeroninstruction.org/files/Why%20Teach%20Spelling.pdf
- Horobin, S. (2013). *Does spelling matter?* Oxford, UK: Oxford University Press.
- *Five questions teachers ask about spelling:* An Interview with J. Richard Gentry. Zaner-Bloser website at: https://www.zaner-bloser.com/news/five-questions-teachers-ask-about-spelling
- Valuable material on a number of different spelling issues can be located at: http:// www.putlearningfirst.com/language/02signs/spell.html

Chapter 2

Visual and visual-motor aspects of spelling

Spelling is much more than a purely 'mechanical' skill; it involves the integration of complex perceptual and cognitive (brain-based) processes (Santoro, Coyne and Simmons, 2006). In particular, efficient visual and auditory processing abilities are essential for learning, remembering and encoding words correctly.

Neuroscientists have long debated whether the ability to spell relies more on applying phonic knowledge or on memorizing visual images of words as wholes. These processes are executed by different, but closely linked, areas of the brain. Evidence from functional magnetic resonance imaging (fMRI) suggests that both processes play important and complementary roles (Norton, Kovelman and Petitto, 2007). Due attention therefore needs to be given during instruction to both visual and auditory aspects of word structure (Khamsi, 2007; Schroeder, 1968). This chapter explains the role and importance of visual and visual-motor processes. The following chapter deals in detail with auditory functions.

Visual perception

To a significant extent we do learn to spell 'by eye', and visual skills are intimately involved in spelling and proofreading (Davis, 2013). Indeed, in the past some experts have placed the greatest importance on visual perception, believing that spelling is a strictly visual process (Hendrickson, 1967; Peters, 1970; 1985). These writers even suggest that attending to sounds within words, and using auditory information when spelling, can lead to disaster with the English language. However, more recent research strongly counter-balances this viewpoint by highlighting the crucial role of auditory perception in spelling (Levy, 2011).

For the vast majority of learners in school, visual perception is usually already adequately developed for the purposes of learning to read, spell and write. It must be emphasized at this point that weakness in visual processing is rarely the single or main cause of spelling difficulties in children above the age of six. On entry to school, most children simply need to be helped to apply their existing visual skills specifically to working efficiently with words in print. However, as Holland (2012) points out, for just a few children visual difficulties can impact on how well they use visualization and visual recall in learning to recognize and encode words. Those with visual problems may find it difficult to recall a word as an accurate image, and thus have problems building up a sight vocabulary of everyday words. When writing, these children may make careless or inconsistent errors, with some letters transposed or omitted. They may also have difficulties identifying these errors when they proofread their written work. It is argued sometimes that vision is not the strongest channel for learning in just a few normal students (Adams-Gordon, 2010a). These students usually benefit from an approach to learning that can also draw on other sensory modalities, as described later under multisensory methods.

The National Center for Learning Disabilities in the US identifies several visual processes that are involved to varying degrees, and at different stages, in learning to spell (NCLD, 2008). The key processes include visual discrimination, visual sequential memory, and visual-motor coordination. In cases of severe spelling disability, weakness in any of these processes may be a contributory factor.

Visual discrimination

Visual discrimination is the most basic skill we use in spelling, to differentiate among different letters of the alphabet and to note subtle differences in spelling patterns. A learner must be able to see and remember these differences and apply them when writing. According to Puranik, Lonigan and Kim (2011), spelling may be regarded as a developmental skill that begins in preschool and incorporates early letter recognition, letter formation and print knowledge.

As long ago as 1949, Hudson and Toler confirmed the importance of visual discrimination in learning to read and spell. More than two decades of research followed, exploring the effectiveness of training visual perception as a means of overcoming problems with word recognition and spelling. As a result, during the 1960s and 1970s many teaching resources were published that claimed to improve learners' visual skills in a general way (e.g., *Frostig Visual-Perceptual Training Program*: Frostig and Horne, 1964; *Visual-Perceptual Training Program*: Breslauer *et al.*, 1976). It was common to find that these training materials involved working only with pictures, patterns and shapes rather than with letters and words. The eventual outcomes from such 'process training' were disappointing in terms of reading and spelling (Anderson and Stern, 1972; Keesbury, 2007). While students undergoing the prescribed training usually did show improvement in the activities involved in the programme, there was very little (if any) transfer and generalization to the recognition or spelling of words. Process training is therefore no longer regarded as best practice. Later studies have indicated that to improve an individual's ability to spell, all activities must focus from the start on working with letters and words, not with abstract shapes, pictures and patterns.

Visual sequential memory

Visual sequential memory is involved in storing and remembering groups of letters in their correct order, in printed, typed and handwritten words. It is a key component in the ability to recall correct visual images of words and syllables, and to identify errors when proofreading. Visual memory helps to compensate for an over-dependence on spelling words purely phonetically. For example, it is visual memory for letter sequences that helps a speller recognize that the word '*street*' is not written as 'streat' or 'strete', even though these alternatives sound equally plausible when the word is spoken. Rutner (2012) points out that effective visual imagery and visual memory help learners deal with the irregularities that do occur in English spelling. However, Moats (2009) points out that spelling involves much more than visual memory.

Over a period of time, young learners store in visual memory the letter sequences that represent common everyday words that need to be instantly recognized and written or typed automatically (e.g., 'the', 'was', 'said', 'they'). Equally important, learners must begin to store and remember visual images of common letter sequences that represent pronounceable parts of longer and more complex words—sequences such as: *str–, pho–, gra–, pre–, –tion, –eet, –eal, –ally, –ist, –ence, –tch, –ck, –ay*. This represents a major step forward in their acquisition of orthographic knowledge. Linguists refer to these important letter sequences as 'sub-lexical sound-spelling correspondences' (McCloskey, 2009). The importance of helping learners master these units for both reading and spelling purposes is discussed in more detail in Chapter 7.

Visual-motor coordination and handwriting

Visual-motor coordination refers here not only to eye movements when viewing words in print, but also to using the eyes effectively to control the direction, size and shape of letters as a word is written. In the case of proficient writers this motor process becomes entirely automatic, but younger children are still bringing the necessary hand-eye coordination skills under control for writing purposes.

It has long been believed that handwriting plays an important part in becoming an accurate speller. Not that there is necessarily a direct cause–effect relationship between good handwriting and accurate spelling; but being able to produce handwriting easily and smoothly frees up the writer to focus much more on the correct spelling of the words. Children with learning difficulties often have problems developing an easy and automatic writing style, and this causes them to focus too much attention and effort on the purely mechanical aspects. They also spend more time processing and checking the spelling of words as they write, which slows down their overall writing performance and output (Sumner, Connelly and Barnett, 2013).

Many years ago Frith (1982) remarked that automaticity in spelling involves the easy written reproduction of sequences of letters that occur in words and in word-components (i.e., the sub-lexical sound-spelling correspondences referred to above). Similarly, Peters (1974) regarded accurate spelling as being heavily dependent upon the formation of correct 'motor habits' that establish a stock of letter sequences in orthographic memory. And Nichols (1985) even suggested that the spelling pattern of a word is remembered best in the movements that are required to write it. This type of kinaesthetic memory of letter sequences is what eventually enables handwriting and spelling to become swift and automatic for most learners. The same is true of typing words on a keyboard. Once a word has been written or typed many times it is firmly stored as a motor memory, and the writing process becomes much more automatic.

It is widely recognized that weak spellers at any age often use poor handwriting as a cover for their difficulties with spelling. There exists the apocryphal story of the teacher who, when writing the annual report for a student, entered a comment under 'Spelling': 'I do not know if he is a good or bad speller, because it is impossible to read his handwriting.'

Groff (1995) cited studies that suggest the style of handwriting children use, whether *cursive* (joined) or *manuscript* (each letter written separately) does not significantly affect their spelling ability. This view is in direct contrast to that of some experts who believe that children find it easier to learn to spell if they are taught cursive style from the beginning (Cripps, 1990; Peters, 1985; Stirling, 2011a). According to Montgomery (2012, p.134):

> the major advantage of cursive [is] the fact that each word or syllable consists of one continuous line where all the elements flow together. This means that the child experiences more readily the total form or shape of a given word as he or she monitors the kinaesthetic feedback from the writing movements. Handwriting therefore supports spelling and this contributes to literacy development.

Best practices

- Any classroom programme for teaching children to spell must include learning activities that help develop visual and visual-motor skills necessary for processing words effectively.
- These activities for developing children's visual skills must involve working with letters and letter sequences.
- When children are studying words, teachers should make effective use of visual methods of presentation, such as underlining tricky parts of a word, using colour to highlight particular letter clusters, and using flashcards to display irregular words that need to be mastered by sight.
- From the earliest stages of schooling children should be taught a smooth and easy style of handwriting as an aid to spelling development.
- Multisensory teaching approaches (including the use of the computer) are helpful in incorporating the use of visual skills.

Online and print resources

- Shelton, L. (undated) *Spelling for mainly visual learners*. http://www.literacynet. org/diversity/spelling.html
- *Spelling using visual skills (2010). Examples for classroom activities.* http://www. skillsworkshop.org/resources/spelling-visual-skills
- *Spelling difficulties in children caused by vision problems.* The Vision Therapy Website at: http://info.thevisiontherapycenter.com/discovering-vision-therapy/ bid/81695/Spelling-Difficulties-in-Children-Caused-by-Vision-Problems

Chapter 3

Auditory and phonological aspects of spelling

A speller needs to be able to hear spoken words clearly (auditory acuity), identify the separate sound units (phonemes) making up the words (phonemic awareness), and possess the necessary knowledge to represent these sounds with correct letters and groups of letters (phonic knowledge). A speller also needs to be able to pronounce words accurately in speech—which depends partly on auditory discrimination but also on self-monitoring, feedback and correction from the language environment.

Accurate auditory processing is absolutely essential when spoken words are to be translated into written words. Most children need to be taught how to take words apart mentally, because this is not necessarily a natural or automatic language process. In everyday communication one does not need to take words apart in order to learn to speak or listen. Speaking and listening skills are acquired more holistically, by immersion in a language environment. For most young children, the specific auditory skills required in reading and in spelling need to be taught and practised. These skills are described below.

Auditory discrimination

Auditory discrimination is the ability to detect similarities and differences between words, and between the phonemes they contain; for example, being able to detect the difference between the spoken words 'thirteen' and 'thirty', and between the sounds /f/, /th/, and /v/ (as in *finger*, *thumb* and *velvet*). Weak auditory discrimination skills can cause problems with accurate pronunciation of words in speech, which in turn affects spelling (McCabe, 1997). [See also *auditory-vocal skills* below]

Phonemic awareness

Phonemic awareness refers to the ability to focus upon the separate sounds within words—an ability fundamental to understanding the relationship between written and spoken language. Phonemic awareness combines auditory discrimination and an ability to take words apart mentally and blend sounds together for reading and spelling purposes. A broader term, *phonological awareness,* includes the ability to break sentences down into words, and words into syllables and constituent sounds. Phonological awareness also includes the ability to detect words that rhyme.

Phonemic awareness appears to be a crucial factor underpinning early reading and spelling (Fletcher-Flinn, Elmes and Strugnell, 1997; Melby-Lervåg, Lyster and Hulme,

2012) and it remains a very strong predictor of spelling ability through the ages up to young adult (Crowley, Mayer and Stuart-Hamilton, 2009). Research has confirmed that developing phonemic awareness must be an essential focus in all early literacy teaching (Yeung, Siegel and Chan, 2013). This can be achieved for most young children simply through fun activities that arouse their interest in 'playing with sounds' and thinking actively about words as a prelude to commencement of more formal phonics instruction. Activities typically provided in early literacy teaching include: playing with rhymes, isolating initial sounds in words, blending sounds to make words, and breaking words down into sound units (segmentation). For example, Mann, Bushell and Morris (2010) have shown experimentally that teaching young children to attend to the sounds within words, phoneme-by-phoneme, leads to an improvement in their emerging spelling ability.

Many students with reading and spelling difficulties exhibit significant weaknesses in phonemic and phonological awareness (Atkins and Tierney, 2004; Moats, 2009; Schäffler et al., 2004). However, there is evidence to indicate that this weakness can be overcome through specific training (e.g., Ball and Blachman, 1991; Bus and Van Ijzendoorn, 1999; Carroll et al., 2003; Maslanka and Joseph, 2002; Stuart, 1999). These studies also indicate that the impact of phonemic awareness training is maximized when it is combined with the direct teaching of letter-sound relationships (the beginning of phonics).

Unlike the poor results obtained from the direct training of visual perception that was attempted in the 1960s, studies in the 1980s began to provide clear evidence that training auditory skill in parallel with teaching letter-to-sound correspondences produces positive gains in both reading and spelling (Bradley and Bryant, 1983; Santoro, Coyne and Simmons, 2006; Tangel and Blachman, 1995).

Phonic knowledge

The overwhelming consensus that has emerged from research in recent years is that, in order to read and spell with confidence, all children aged five to six years should begin to receive systematic teaching that develops their knowledge of letter-to-sound relationships (Adams, 1990; de Graaff et al., 2009; Lonigan and Shanahan, 2008; Rose, 2009; Torgerson et al., 2006; Treiman, Stothard and Snowling, 2013). Children cannot become independent readers and spellers unless they master the alphabetic code. Studies have indicated clearly that explicit teaching of phonics in the early school years produces better results than relying merely on incidental learning (Adams, 1990; Rose, 2009; Vadasy and Sanders, 2013).

So far, research evidence suggests that the method known as *synthetic phonics* (teaching letter-to-sound correspondences first, and then building words by blending these sounds) produces the best results (DET [NSW] 2009; Hepplewhite, 2008; Johnston and Watson, 2003). Synthetic phonics helps children acquire decoding and encoding strategies that they can then apply independently. Most teachers using this phonic approach in the First Grade find that 10 to 20 minutes a day spent in enjoyable decoding and encoding activities enables young children to master the fundamental relationships between letters and sounds.

While students do need specific time devoted to mastering phonic units and working with word families (see Chapter 7), every effort must be made to ensure that this knowledge is quickly applied to meaningful everyday reading and writing. Phonic skills should not be taught and practised totally out of context. It is therefore helpful to provide young children with reading books that have been controlled for word difficulty and that deliberately contain a majority of regular words that can be decoded and encoded easily. At one period during the 1980s and 1990s these graded phonics books fell out of favour with teachers using the whole-language approach. Fortunately, the value of using decodable material with beginning readers and writers has again been recognized.

Teaching phonics

There is no prescribed order in which to introduce letter-to-sound correspondences; but it is useful to consider how the task might be organized into a logical sequence. One effective approach is to begin with highly contrastive sounds such as /k/, /b/, /m/, /v/ and avoiding confusable sounds such as /w/ and /r/, /m/ and /n/, or /p/ and /b/. The following consonants can provide a useful starting point because they are consistent in representing only one sound, regardless of the letter or letters coming after them in a word: j, k, l, m, n, p, b, h, r, v, w. Vowels are much less consistent than consonants in the sounds they represent. Most teachers begin by first establishing the most common vowel sound associations (/a/ as in *apple*, /e/ as in *egg*, /i/ as in *ink*, /o/ as in *orange* and /u/ as in *up*) and then using these in simple word building and spelling activities. More difficult vowel units are best tackled later, when they appear in combination with other letters (e.g., –ar–, –aw–, –ie–, –ee–, –ea–, –ai–). It is at this point that teachers also need to check that children are producing these sounds clearly and accurately, as this will affect their ability to sound out, blend, and spell words correctly.

Although it is obviously possible for teachers simply to use their own knowledge of spelling and phonics to devise a programme of instruction, there are also many commercial programmes available to help them, including THRASS (*Teaching Handwriting, Reading and Spelling Skills*: Davies, 2006), *Jolly Phonics* (Lloyd and Lib, 2000), *Go Phonics* (Davison, 2001), *Saxon Phonics and Spelling K–3* (Saxon Publishing, 2004) and *Letterland* (Wendon, 2006). All of these programmes introduce phonic units and spelling patterns in a sequenced manner, and provide a range of activities that help reinforce learning. Computer software for students and teachers is now associated with most of these programmes; and teachers can also find much valuable material through simple online searches using the key words 'phonics' and 'teaching phonics'.

As indicated in Chapter 1, it is important for both reading (word recognition) and spelling purposes that children progress quickly beyond single-letter decoding to recognizing and using letter groups that represent functional components within words (e.g., –ate, as in *date*, *sk–ate*, *pl–ate*, *de–bate*, *re–tal–i–ate*) and that also comprise rhyme units, prefixes or suffixes. Word study activities that help to expand learners' repertoire of phonic encoding skills are discussed in Chapter 7.

Auditory memory

Recalling the correct spelling of a word relies on remembering the phonemes and syllables in the exact order in which they occur within the word. This is referred to more specifically as 'auditory *sequential* memory' (Goldstein and Schwebach, 2009).

Spelling errors often reflect a failure to recall and encode constituent sounds in the correct order (e.g., 'remember' written as 'rmember', or 'wrold' for 'world'). A method called Exaggerated Pronunciation (Over Articulation) can be helpful for strengthening auditory memory for letter sequences (see Chapter 6).

Auditory attention

Associated closely with auditory memory is auditory *attention*. A student is much more likely to store the sounds within a word in the correct order if he or she is deliberately attending to the word with every intention of remembering and reproducing it accurately (Westwood, 2006). One essential feature of any attempt to improve spelling must be the use of materials and tasks that engage a student's full interest and hold attention effectively.

Auditory-vocal skills

As indicated at several points already, clear and accurate speech plays an important role in spelling (Papen, Watson and Marriot, 2012; Scott and Brown, 2001). For example, Rosenthal and Ehri (2011) have reported on the benefits of having children read new words aloud (rather than processing them silently) when encountering them for the first time in an unfamiliar text. This appears to strengthen connections between the spellings and their pronunciation.

In cases of serious spelling difficulty it is wise to check if the speller is actually hearing and pronouncing a target word correctly. For example, you are unlikely to spell *Antarctic* correctly if you say '*Antartic*', *clothes* if you say '*close*', *animal* if you say '*aminal*', *escape* if you say '*excape*', or *library* if you say '*libary*'. The issue of accurate pronunciation is particularly relevant when teaching English as a second language, but also applies to students from restricted language backgrounds, those using a strong regional dialect, and students with hearing impairment.

It is clear from what has been discussed in this chapter that teaching children to apply their listening skills must be an essential component of any spelling instruction provided in school or tutorial centres.

Best practices

- Any classroom programme for teaching children to spell must include learning activities that help develop auditory skills necessary for processing and encoding words effectively.
- In the early stages of all literacy programmes, children need to be taught how to play with sounds within words and how to blend sounds to form words.
- The most effective beginning literacy approach combines phonological training (and, where necessary, speech training) with the teaching of letter-to-sound correspondences and decoding.
- The synthetic phonics approach is currently considered the most effective for developing early reading and spelling skills.
- Multisensory teaching approaches that involve a combination of visual, auditory and kinaesthetic input (VAK) are often helpful, particularly with the weakest spellers.

Online and print resources

- Information on phonemic and phonological awareness can be located on the Reading Rockets website at: http://www.readingrockets.org/helping/target/phonologicalphonemic/
- The following URL will take you to the abstract from a report on improving auditory discrimination with dyslexic students. Schäffler, T., Sonntag, J., Hartnegg, K. and Fischer, B. (2004). The effect of practice on low-level auditory discrimination, phonological skills, and spelling in dyslexia. *Dyslexia, 10,* 2: 119-30. http://www.ncbi.nlm.nih.gov/pubmed/15180393
- The abstract for another study with learning disabled students can be located at the URL below. Atkins, M. and Tierney, E. (2004) Memory skills and specific learning difficulties. *Research Journal of Special Needs in Ireland, 17,* 2: 81-92: http://www.fedvol.ie/The_Relationship_Between_Memory_Skills_Auditory_and_Visual_and_Reading_and_Spelling_Ability_for_a_Sample_of_Children_with_Specific_Learning_Disabilities/Default.1226.html
- The Good Schools Guide website has an item called *Ten factors that may indicate an Auditory Processing Disorder (APD).* http://www.goodschoolsguide.co.uk/help-and-advice/special-needs-advice/types-of-sen/sensory-difficulties/204/auditory-processing-difficulties

Chapter 4

Cognitive and metacognitive aspects of spelling

Cognition is the faculty humans possess for processing information, thinking, responding, and deliberately applying knowledge or skills. The term *cognitive* is applied to all mental processes that involve attending, remembering, reasoning, language comprehension, problem solving, and decision making. *Metacognition* refers to the ability to think about and control one's own cognitive processes. This is often termed 'thinking about your own thinking', and is an essential part of self-monitoring.

As stated in Chapter 1, spelling is essentially a 'thinking process' (Johnson, 1998; Roberts, 2001; Tompkins, 2010a). The human brain enables a writer to integrate and apply different sources of information (visual, phonological, orthographic, kinaesthetic and morphological) that contribute to word recognition and proficient spelling (Steffler, 2001; Treiman and Cassar, 1997). For example, careful thinking is required when analysing and storing information about a word, and when recalling relevant aspects later when encoding the word. When an individual is writing, proofreading, or correcting errors, he or she must consciously judge the correctness of the visual appearance of the written word, and must weigh up alternative ways of representing sound and meaning in that word (Dich and Pedersen, 2013; Draper, 2008; Scott-Dunne, 2012; Topfer and Arendt, 2009). Cognitive skills are also directly involved in developing and applying appropriate mental strategies for learning words, and for recognizing useful connections between words.

This chapter describes the role of cognition and metacognition in developing effective learning strategies, understanding spelling rules, and in developing at least a working awareness of morphology. Research-based teaching and learning activities covering these important areas are described in more detail in later chapters.

Cognitive strategies

Learning to spell correctly necessitates the use of several appropriate cognitive strategies. A cognitive strategy can be thought of as a *mental plan of action* over which an individual can exercise control when tackling a particular task or problem in a systematic manner. The brain is responsible for devising, selecting, and applying these strategies to suit a specific purpose (e.g., learning to spell an irregular word; correcting an error), and then for monitoring the effectiveness of the strategy (metacognition). Teachers have the responsibility for instructing students in the effective application of spelling strategies (Berninger *et al.*, 2013; Davis, 2013; Tompkins, 2010a).

Competent spellers possess a repertoire of ways for learning, storing, recalling and checking the spelling of the words they use. Less competent spellers, perhaps because of under-developed metacognitive skills, tend to develop fewer strategies and therefore resort to rote learning (Kraai, 2011). Rote learning is, of course, one type of strategy for learning words, but one that automatically limits the learner to acquiring a spelling vocabulary one word at a time. Learning words as single unrelated entities does not help a learner recognize useful connections between spelling patterns across different words. However, rote learning with repeated writing and checking still remains an important way of learning to spell unpredictable (irregular) words.

Research has discovered that the most common spelling strategies learners tend to use at different stages of development include:

- learning a specific spelling pattern by frequently looking at the word (visualizing) and then repeatedly writing it (rote learning);
- rehearsing the spelling of the word by repeating the names of the letters in sequence (often referred to as 'simultaneous oral spelling');
- using phonic knowledge to segment and then encode the word, or an approximation to the word, by attending to component sounds (phonetic spelling);
- using knowledge of the spelling of another word that sounds a little like (or rhymes with) the target word (spelling by analogy);
- applying spelling *rules* in conjunction with any of the above strategies;
- creating easy-to-remember mnemonics to help recall tricky words (e.g., *'because'*— Big Elephants Can Always Understand Small Elephants; *'ocean'*—Our Cuddly Elephants Are Nice);
- applying knowledge of word meanings, derivations, prefixes, and suffixes (morphemic approach);
- using a dictionary and/or computer spell-checker;
- asking a superior speller for help.

Studies have shown that the range of strategies children use increases steadily with age, starting usually with the first three approaches listed above. However, the progression is not entirely linear, and children in the primary school years use multiple strategies, often resorting to unsophisticated and inefficient methods if faced with difficult words (Harrison, 2005; Ralston and Robinson, 1997; Rittle-Johnson and Siegler, 1999; Sharp, Sinatra and Reynolds, 2008). In a study of students' spelling errors in Grades 1 to 9, Bahr *et al.* (2012) conclude that normal spelling development is nonlinear, and it takes a long time to develop a robust orthographic lexicon that coordinates phonology, orthography, and morphology in support of conventional spelling.

Spelling rules

Among the several contributions that cognition makes to spelling is the ability to learn (or absorb incidentally) basic spelling rules—such as dropping the 'y' in a word like *'rely'* when it becomes *'relies'* or *'reliable'*, or doubling a single consonant, for example when *'rob'* becomes *'robbed'*. There are many such rules in English and just a few of these are summarized in Appendix A7. However, it must be emphasized here that *the vast majority of students do not learn to spell simply by being taught a set of rules.*

In general, research has not shown the formal teaching of spelling rules to be an effective instructional method—although several anecdotal and case-study accounts (particularly from older students with learning disabilities) have suggested that learning rules helped them combat a spelling weakness (Darch *et al.*, 2000; Massengill, 2006).

Many rules are very complicated, and may apply only to a very small number of words. There are so many exceptions to almost every rule that there is limited value in devoting too much time and attention to the explicit teaching of such rules. The linguist Richard Nordquist (2012) has rightly observed that:

> Spelling rules are a bit like weather forecasts: we may use them, but we really can't depend on them to be right 100% of the time. In fact, the only fool-proof rule is that all spelling rules in English have exceptions (n.p.).

There may be a place, however, for teaching rules to intelligent students with dyslexia, as part of the repertoire of self-help strategies that they need to use when proofreading and correcting their errors (Kemper, Verhoeven and Bosman, 2012; White, 2012). However, automatic transfer of such learning to students' everyday writing and spelling is often negligible.

Students with learning difficulties have the greatest problem remembering and applying spelling rules. It is best instead to teach these students effective strategies for learning new target words and for proofreading, rather than attempting to teach obscure rules that are unlikely to be remembered or understood (Watson, 2013). For example, it is almost impossible to remember a rule such as 'when adding a vowel suffix to a closed syllable, double the final consonant (to keep the vowel sound short) before adding the suffix (e.g. *shop* to *shop* + *p* + *ing*)'. It is easier simply to teach thoroughly the word *shopping*, while pointing out to the learner that we must always add the extra *p* (word-specific knowledge). Frequent reminders are usually necessary when teachers are providing constructive feedback on written assignments. Students can also be helped to develop an awareness of similar words that require a double letter through specific word-study activities (e.g., *travel/travelling, hop/hopping, knit/ knitting, pot/potted*). They can also be taught the self-prompting strategy of asking themselves 'Do I need to double the middle letter in this word?' whenever they check through their written work.

If a teacher does decide to embody the teaching of rules within a spelling approach, this should not begin too early in the children's school life. It seems that children first need to establish a foundation of word-specific knowledge on which to build later an understanding of rules (Chliounaki and Bryant, 2007; Sanchez, Magnan and Ecalle, 2012).

Other information on spelling rules can be located in the sources listed at the end of this chapter and in the Appendix.

Morphology

Morphological information refers to the meanings of component parts of words (morphemes) and the way in which words are reconstructed as meaning changes (e.g., *joy* can become *joyful, enjoy, enjoys, enjoyment, enjoying, enjoyed, enjoyable*). Morphemes (units of meaning) are the building blocks for creating spelling patterns.

An awareness of morphology involves recognizing root words, compound words (like *volleyball*), prefixes and suffixes (such as *pre–, un–, non–, –ing, –est, –ed, –ier*) and—at a much higher level—the origin and derivations of words (etymology). Morphology also includes the rules that predict how spelling patterns change as the meaning or inflection of a word changes.

The brain is responsible for comprehending and storing morphological aspects of word knowledge. While the human brain can deduce some morphological information through constant exposure to words in meaningful contexts, studies suggest that this is an area of word study that can be enhanced considerably by explicit instruction (Arndt, 2010; Arndt and Foorman, 2009; Devonshire, Morris and Fluck, 2013; Diaz, 2010; Vitale, Medland and Kaniuka, 2010). Several ways in which such instruction can be provided are described in Chapter 7.

The highest level of cognition is concerned with thinking about derivation of words and parts of words as an aid to their spelling. This highest level of understanding is attained by very few students today, mainly because it is rarely the focus of any teaching currently provided in our schools (Arndt and Foorman, 2009; Carlisle, 2010). Applying rules and using morphological information remain the least used cognitive strategies, even by older learners. It has been suggested that schools need to give more attention to teaching children effective spelling strategies and raising their awareness of morphological aspects of the words they encounter (Arndt, 2010; Carlisle, 2010; Dahl *et al.*, 2003).

Reading and spelling: reciprocal influences

One complex cognitive skill closely associated with spelling is, of course, text reading. It is obvious that frequent reading is the chief means by which learners are exposed to orthographic patterns. When an individual is reading text, many of the cognitive processes involved in recognizing words and constructing meaning are similar to the processes required when spelling. Spelling and reading are thus mutually supportive activities (Ehri, 1997; Montgomery, 2005; Santoro, Coyne and Simmons, 2006). Spelling helps to strengthen reading by reinforcing the utility of phonic knowledge, and by establishing commonly occurring letter sequences. Reading helps spelling by exposing the reader to a wide variety of orthographic patterns, and by building a vocabulary of common sight words (including irregular words). Reading also provides opportunities for applying phonic decoding skills that are used in reverse when encoding words. However, Norton *et al.* (2007) have remarked that, 'Little is known [still] about how the capacity to spell relates to the overall reading process, and how spelling may contribute to the acquisition and promotion of successful reading and language processes' (p.48).

Research has tended to support a view that ongoing experiences with reading contribute to an individual's ability to spell (Burt and Fury, 2000; Conrad, 2008; Ehri, 2000; Krashen, 2002; Templeton and Morris, 2001), but reading skills tend to develop well ahead of spelling skills. The correlation between reading and spelling has been reported to be in the moderate to high range (between 0.68 and 0.86) (Arndt and Foorman, 2009). However, reading and spelling are not simply mirror images of the same process. While studies using fMRI have revealed that reading and spelling share some specific areas of the brain (Norton, Kovelman and Petitto, 2007; Rapp and

Lipka, 2011), spelling ability (encoding) demands certain knowledge and specific skills that are not used—or are used differently—when reading (decoding) (Moats, 2005). The brain is responsible for utilizing those aspects of reading ability that are helpful for spelling, and vice versa. If the connection between reading and spelling was perfect, all good readers would be good spellers—and this is manifestly not the case; some very good readers and writers are weak spellers (Moats, 2005).

The message for teachers is that teaching children to read will not automatically ensure that they learn to spell (Holmes and Babauta, 2005). Alongside reading, spelling skills and strategies need to be explicitly taught as thinking processes, with corrective feedback as necessary (Rippel, 2013). Methods for teaching spelling alongside reading are described in the next two chapters.

Best practices

- From the very beginning, spelling needs to be taught as a thinking process.
- Studies have supported the value of teaching students effective mental strategies to use when writing, spelling and proofreading.
- Direct and explicit teaching of these mental strategies is preferable to hoping that students will discover or invent them independently.
- Like all forms of strategy training, it will usually take longer than teachers expect for students to adopt spelling strategies and use them independently.
- Programmes that are based on teaching and drilling spelling rules are rarely effective; but reference can be made to some common rules with few exceptions when discussing written work with individual students.
- Basic morphological principles should be taught to students in upper primary and secondary schools, as part of learning about language.

Online and print resources

- *Effective spelling strategies*. http://www.allaboutlearningpress.com/effective-spelling-strategies
- Snowball, D. *Spelling strategies: Make smart use of sounds and spelling patterns*. http://teacher.scholastic.com/lessonrepro/lessonplans/instructor/spell4.htm
- Department of Education, South Australia. (2000). *Spelling strategies: Secret weapons for spelling*. http://www.decd.sa.gov.au/curric/files/pages/saisop/Vacation Literacy/spsmain.htm
- A few useful rules for spelling are summarized on the website maintained by Amity Reading Clubs at: http://www.amity.org.uk/Training/Spelling%20Rules/Spelling%20Rules.htm
- Stowe, M. (2013). *Teaching morphology: Enhancing vocabulary development and reading comprehension*. http://education.wm.edu/centers/ttac/resources/articles/teachtechnique/teachingmorphology/index.php

Chapter 5

General principles for teaching spelling

The previous chapters described the visual, auditory, kinaesthetic, cognitive and metacognitive underpinnings of learning spelling. This chapter, and those that follow, discuss effective methods for teaching spelling that take account of these factors and are supported by research evidence.

Basic principles

From the many studies of teaching spelling that have been conducted over the years there is consensus that, in addition to constant exposure to words through daily reading and writing, it is also necessary to provide students with *explicit instruction* (Adams-Gordon, 2010b; Gagen, 2010; Graham, 1999; Moats, 2005). One essential component of effective instruction already referred to is teaching students *cognitive strategies* for tackling new words and for checking and self-correcting (Hepplewhite, 2008; Watson, 2013).

There is also unanimous agreement that there is no substitute for regular practice and frequent revision of words that have been studied (Gagen, 2010). For this reason, instructional programmes need to revisit and consolidate previously taught material, thus deepening and extending spelling knowledge (Davis, 2013). It is also agreed that instruction and learning activities in spelling must take due account of the stage of linguistic development that the children have reached (Templeton and Morris, 2001; Tompkins, 2010a). The developmental stages in spelling are clearly described later in Chapter 8.

Classroom research suggests that adequate teaching time (at least 15 minutes a day in the early primary years) needs to be allocated for spelling instruction and practice (Moats, 2005; Rippel, 2013). For example, Hepplewhite (2008, p.1) has stated that if schools have '... a regular ring-fenced spot on the timetable (daily at first reducing to twice a week when appropriate), then spelling can definitely be taught well and pupils can definitely make improvements.' Unfortunately, it seems that, with an overloaded curriculum, teachers find it increasingly difficult to devote the necessary time and attention (Manning and Tibshraeny, 2013). Perhaps the challenge is always greatest for teachers in upper primary and secondary schools, who must remember to set aside appropriate lesson time each week to address students' spelling progress. Subject specialist teachers in secondary schools need to take particular note of this requirement.

Characteristics of an effective programme

Drawing on the available research data on teaching spelling, an effective approach clearly involves:

- arousing children's interest in words and in spelling;
- allocating specific time for instruction, practice, proofreading and self-correction;
- matching materials and activities to students' stage of development;
- teaching a core vocabulary of high-frequency words to mastery level;
- teaching students cognitive strategies for tackling words;
- making classroom resources readily available that enable spellers to 'help themselves' when writing (dictionaries, common core word lists, topic-specific word lists, Word Walls, computer access).

Role of the teacher

The teacher is the key to an effective spelling programme, and his or her genuine enthusiasm for words should motivate children to become equally interested and engaged (Davis, 2013). The important role of the teacher is to encourage students to develop an attitude that accurate spelling is important, and that it is something that can be achieved through their own efforts.

Teachers also need to be able to demonstrate (model) efficient strategies for learning and recalling words and for proofreading, checking and self-correcting (Hepplewhite, 2008). Teachers represent the most useful source of corrective feedback to students, so regular correction of students' written work remains an important professional duty. Monitoring and checking students as they write provides an opportunity for constructive advice to spellers, tailored to the needs of each individual student. Studies suggest that correcting and discussing errors during the lesson is more effective than handing back marked assignments several days later (Gentry, 1987).

Teaching approaches

There are several classroom approaches to teaching and learning spelling (Schlagal, 2002). These can be summarized as:

- *immersion and incidental learning*—'catch' spelling as you read and write;
- *cognitive strategy training*—direct teaching that informs students how best to learn words, or attempt to spell unfamiliar words;
- *word study*—examining the meaning and significance of words and parts of words, and understanding how words are constructed;
- *published spelling programmes and lists*—the 'basal speller' approach.

Immersion and incidental learning

This unstructured approach was extremely popular during the two decades of the 'whole-language' teaching in primary classrooms. The thinking at the time was that children should be encouraged to write freely without the constraints of needing to spell words correctly (Gentry, 1978). Children were encouraged to invent the spelling of any words they wanted to use, and teachers did not believe in providing too much correction (Lutz, 1986). They might sometimes help an individual child with a word he or she wanted to write; or they might occasionally provide a mini lesson to the group on a particular spelling rule or pattern. But there was no explicit instruction provided on how to learn words, and no real effort was made to teach a core vocabulary of words required for everyday writing. More recently, this incidental learning approach is seen to be too lacking in structure, too weak in intensity, and quite likely to develop a belief in young writers that 'spelling doesn't matter' (Groff, 2007). In particular, this unstructured approach disadvantages students with learning difficulties who most require direct teaching.

Cognitive strategy training

Teaching children strategies (the 'how to') for spelling is far more important than simply providing the correct spelling of a specific word when they require it (Montgomery, 2005). As explained earlier, a cognitive strategy is a mental plan of action that enables an individual to approach a task like spelling in a rational and efficient manner. Often a cognitive strategy can be taught in the form of a simple 'mental script' that an individual can draw upon when needed. The script directs the learner to think logically and respond appropriately at each stage in spelling and checking a word. Examples are provided in the next chapter.

Teachers have a key responsibility to teach such cognitive strategies by demonstrating the approach very clearly by 'thinking aloud' at each step, then giving students abundant opportunities to use the strategy independently.

Word study

Educators came to realize that there are definite limits to what can be achieved through rote memorization for learning to spell. A more powerful approach that emerged in the 1990s involves teaching not only strategies for learning and checking spellings, but also showing students how and why words are constructed in specific ways (Abbott, 2001; Moats, 2005; Rasinski and Zutell, 2010). With this additional morphemic knowledge, the spelling of words becomes much more predictable and rational. According to Leipzig (2000, p.1), 'Word study provides students with opportunities to investigate and understand the patterns in words, [and] knowledge of these patterns means that students needn't learn to spell one word at a time.'

Chapter 7 is devoted to the important topic of word study as a powerful approach to improving students' spelling skills and insights.

Spelling programmes and lists

Teachers in the United States tend to rely quite heavily on published spelling programmes (basals) containing lists of words grouped into sets appropriate for different age groups (Fresch, 2003). Their students are taken through the weekly lessons to learn these words; and a test at the end of the week acts as the criterion for assessing progress. Associated activities usually include workbook exercises requiring students to write the words, define them, and use them appropriately in sentences. Each lesson may, for example, teach a particular word family, phonic unit, or spelling rule. Some programmes are thematic and organize their words according to given topics or subject matter, rather than phonic principles. However, many commercially published programmes contain no coverage at all of morphemic principles, and relatively little on compound words, homonyms, contractions, and words that are easily confused (Mullock, 2012).

The advocates for the use of published programmes believe that systematic coverage of weekly word groups, together with regular testing, helps students internalize target words and the spelling patterns they represent. Schlagal (2002, p.46) actually states:

> The contemporary basal speller is the result of a long history of research and study. If used appropriately, it offers teachers an efficient and manageable tool that can assist them in teaching their students key elements in the structure of English orthography.

Although basal spelling programmes of this sort are often criticized quite harshly for teaching spelling out of the context of daily authentic writing, these programmes, in the hands of effective teachers, have been shown to produce superior results compared to those obtained by immersion and individual feedback methods (Bruck *et al.*, 1998). Gentry (2000) points out that a good spelling basal is simply a curriculum resource for teaching. He suggests that beginning teachers, and others who have not received extensive training in how best to teach spelling, need this kind of resource, with its clearly defined content and objectives.

Regardless of whether teachers rely on a published programme of some type, or instead adopt their own approach to spelling instruction, it is vital that they have a sound understanding of the English spelling system, the stages of development in becoming a competent speller, and the teaching and learning approaches that have proved to be most effective.

Contribution of technology

For many years, despite fears that spell-checkers would have a negative impact on students' spelling proficiency, it has emerged that this technology can actually aid the development of spelling skills and the writing process, and has greatly facilitated self-correction (Fennema-Jansen, 2001; Hetzroni and Shrieber, 2004; MacArthur *et al.*, 1996; Wanzek *et al.*, 2006).

Recently, there has been a noticeable growth in the use of technology to actually *teach* spelling. For example, in a study conducted by Kast *et al.* (2011) involving the application of spelling training software, children with dyslexia improved their spelling skills to the same extent as children without dyslexia; and they were able to memorize phoneme-to-grapheme correspondences. In addition, the structured and multisensory (auditory, visual, hands-on) aspects of the approach were of benefit to children with poor attention span. Similar support for computer-aided spelling instruction with dyslexic students was found by Ecalle *et al.* (2009). The use of laptops improved the spelling of teenage students with learning disability in a study by Eden, Shamir and Fershtman (2011). Similarly, a study by Wu and Zhang (2010) with Grade 4 students revealed that the students who used handheld computers to learn spelling had significantly higher test scores than students who learned using paper-and-pencil methods.

The use of a word processor with spell-check function has been investigated by Kagohara *et al.* (2012). In their two-case study of adolescents with autism the outcome suggested that the approach was effective in teaching them to check the spelling of words using a common word processing program.

In the next chapter some specific strategies for teaching spelling are described. Computer-based technology can often be incorporated into some of these learning and teaching strategies.

Best practices

- In the most effective classrooms, teachers' own enthusiasm for words (their origins, meanings and spellings) can motivate students to become more interested.
- Effective teachers encourage their students to develop an attitude that accurate spelling is important and can be achieved through their own efforts.
- Specific time must be allocated in the primary school years for instruction and guided practice.
- All students need to master a core vocabulary of high-frequency words.
- Effective instruction in spelling may involve a combination of approaches, including explicit teaching, word study, the use of well-designed published programmes, and computer-based technologies.

Online and print resources

- Watson, S. (2013). *The do's and don'ts of spelling lists*. About.com Special Education website at: http://specialed.about.com/od/literacy/a/spell.htm
- Topfer, C. (2010). *Solving words: A whole-school approach to teaching spelling.* http://midk23.wikispaces.com/file/view/spelling+excellent+C+Topfer+-+Solving+Words.pdf
- TES Connect website (2013). *Spelling Handbook.* http://www.tes.co.uk/teaching-resource/Spelling-Handbook-6039545/
- NSW Department for Education and Communities (2011). *Effective classroom practices.* https://www.artsunit.nsw.edu.au/sites/default/files/Effective_Classroom_Practices.pdf
- Centre for Literacy in Primary Education [UK] (2000). *Understanding spelling.* http://www.clpe.co.uk/research/understanding-spelling

Chapter 6

Specific spelling strategies and interventions

This chapter examines the specific strategies that spellers can be taught to use when attempting to learn and remember words. Darch *et al.* (2000) suggest that it is essential to teach all students effective strategies for tackling words of different types.

Evidence is provided wherever possible to support the inclusion of each strategy as an example of best practice. Most strategies relate not only to studying and learning new words, but also to proofreading and self-correcting errors.

Self-help strategies

One important part of teaching age-appropriate strategies to students is to help them acquire the overall habit of weighing up their options and deciding how best to tackle a word in a given situation. For example, when faced with a new word to learn, students can be taught to say to themselves:

- *Can I spell this word as it sounds?* (Phonetically)
- *Can I break this word down into parts that are easier to spell and remember?* (Segmentation)
- *How many syllables can I hear in this word?*
- *Does this word sound a bit like another word that I can already spell?*
- *Does the word I have written look correct?*
- *This is an irregular word, so I am going to have to write it several times, then underline the tricky part, and remember what the word looks like.*

During any writing or proofreading task, a student might say to herself:

- *Is the word I need to use already listed on the whiteboard?*
- *Can I find the spelling of this word in the online dictionary?*
- *I will write this word three possible ways; then I'll choose the one that looks correct.*
- *I'll write the word as it sounds, then come back and check it when I get to the end.*
- *I'll ask Megan; she's a good speller.*

An effective self-monitoring strategy is extremely valuable to all learners, and usually results in improvement in spelling performance (Cunningham, 2011; Davis, 2013; Wilde, 2007; Zutell, 1979). However, students with learning difficulties often fail to develop effective spelling strategies independently, so they benefit most from explicit strategy instruction.

Students' motivation and attitude are important. Unless they genuinely recognize the value of a particular spelling strategy there is little likelihood that they will continue to use it independently when unsupervised (Darch *et al.*, 2000). Strategy instruction usually takes much longer than teachers anticipate; and students always need to be reminded very frequently to adopt and use a strategy taught previously.

Learning irregular words

The term 'irregular' is commonly used to describe a word with a spelling pattern that does not represent a simple sound-to-letter correspondence. These words are often referred to by teachers as 'tricky words' or—as in the new National Curriculum in the UK—'exception words' (DfE [UK], 2012b). They can be contrasted with 'regular' words in which letters (or letter clusters) consistently represent their common sound.

Many of the irregularities in English spelling are due to the fact that the same sound may be represented by different letters or letter combinations (for example, consider –*ight* and –*ite*, or –*ole*, –*oal*, –*owl*, –*oll*). Or a given letter combination may represent several different sounds (for example, consider the sounds represented by –*ough* in *though, through, rough, thought, bough*, and *thorough*). To complicate matters further, sometimes a letter is 'silent' within a word (*knot, sign, depot*). This problem of irregularity arises because in English there are about 44 different phonemes, but only 26 letters available to represent them. We are forced to use letters in combination, rather than single letters, to represent many speech sounds. As pointed out in Chapter 1, other reasons for irregularity include the fact that some words have been imported into English from other languages, and that a few old words may have originally had a different pronunciation and inconsistent spelling (Crystal, 2011).

There is a temptation to try to teach irregular words as if they can only be learned as whole-word images; but as Reis-Frankfort (2013) points out, spellers should still pay due attention to those parts of an irregular word that can be encoded exactly as they sound, and then concentrate on remembering the 'tricky' parts. In addition, Cooke (1997) suggests that multisensory input should be used when the student is trying to store the structure of an irregular word in memory (e.g., tracing, highlighting, reading the word aloud: see below under *Multisensory Approach*).

There are several strategies that can help in learning the spelling of irregular words. These include Look-Say-Cover-Write-Check, Repeated Writing, Multisensory Approach, Exaggerated Pronunciation (also known as 'Over Articulation'), Simultaneous Oral Spelling (SOS), Mnemonics, and a re-learning procedure known as Old Way/New Way. These strategies are described fully below.

Look-Cover-Write-Check

This visual imagery strategy has been the most widely recommended for learning to spell irregular words, and its efficacy has been investigated in several studies (e.g., Cates *et al.*, 2007; Cooke, 1997; Erion *et al.*, 2009; Fisher, Bruce and Greive, 2007; Jaspers *et al.*, 2012; Keller, 2002; Nies and Belfiore, 2006). Various versions of the strategy exist (e.g., Cover-Write-Check (CWC); Cover-Copy-Compare (CCC); Look-

Say-Cover-Write-Check (LSCWC); Trace-Copy-Recall (TCR); and Spelling with Imagery (SWIM))—but they are all based on the principle of strengthening a learner's use of visualization to store and recall spelling patterns. It is not, of course, an appropriate strategy to use if the target word is perfectly regular and can be encoded simply by attending to letter-sound relationships. This fact is often overlooked in books that recommend the visual imagery strategy for learning *all* words.

The typical steps involved in applying LSCWC are:

- Look carefully at the target word, and say it clearly.
- Use your eyes like a camera and take a picture of the word.
- Close your eyes and imagine you can still see the word.
- Say the word again.
- Trace it in the air, with your eyes still closed.
- Open your eyes and write the word.
- Check the spelling. If necessary correct the word, repeat the steps, and then write the word several times.

Roberts (2012) suggests that teachers should stimulate students' imagery strongly during the visualization stage in the above sequence. He created a modified approach called SWIM in which the teacher or tutor actively promotes visualization of the target word by asking the student to mentally manipulate (play with) the word image in various ways before writing or copying it.

Some online interactive materials using LCWC principles are available. As well as providing a motivating way to help students learn to spell, they often provide teachers with additional ideas for making spelling activities more intrinsically interesting. (See the online and print resources at the end of the chapter.)

In terms of research, Mann, Bushell and Morris (2010) conducted an experiment with primary school students in which they combined CCC with sounding out (SO) of each letter as the child wrote the word. The results suggested that the CCC+SO approach led to good improvement. Another study by Jaspers *et al.* (2012) using children in Grade 1, compared the effectiveness of a simple Cover-Copy-Compare training with a parallel method that combined Cover-Copy-Compare with the experimenter reading aloud a brief definition of the word and a sentence containing the target word. Results showed that both interventions increased participants' spelling ability at a greater rate than a control condition, but there was no obvious advantage of trying to teach the definition in context.

The visual strategy has been found to be effective not only for average learners but also with students with a learning difficulty (Cieslar, McLaughlin and Derby, 2008; Fisher, Bruce and Greive, 2007; Moser *et al.*, 2012; Nies and Belfiore, 2006; Webber, 2009).

Repeated writing

The ultimate value of requiring a student to write a target word or a correction several times depends entirely on the amount of attention the student gives to the task. Often the activity serves no useful purpose because this type of rote performance can be carried out without any cognitive effort (Erion *et al.*, 2009). Usually, the words practised in this way are not stored or remembered later. However, it is a fact that repetition and practice are indispensable procedures for attaining automaticity in any skill domain, including spelling—and even without instruction we usually resort to writing a word more than once if we want to remember it (Gioia, 2008; Morris and Smith, 2011). Repeated writing is one way in which kinaesthetic images of words can be more firmly established. Gagen (2010, p.2) states: 'Writing the word 5–10 times provides the repetition that enhances learning: simple, effective and efficient.'

Repeated writing of a target word can be very helpful indeed if (i) the learner has every intention of trying to remedy an error, and (ii) he or she is attending fully to the task. Only a few words (usually *no more than three*) should be practised in any one tutorial session.

Multisensory Approach

The term 'Multisensory Approach' is most closely associated with such hands-on strategies as finger-tracing over a target word while sounding out the letters, and then writing the word in the air using larger arm movements (sky writing) to reinforce shape and letter sequence (Carreker and Birsh, 2011; Hook and Jones, 2002). But the term multisensory can also be applied to most computer spelling exercises and activities, since they require a combination of looking, listening, typing and self-correction (Kast *et al.*, 2011).

Research has consistently shown that the use of multisensory teaching and learning is extremely helpful for students with learning difficulties, mainly because the approach holds students' full attention and increases their active engagement in learning (Adams-Gordon, 2010a; Logsdon, 2013; Riggs, 2008). Studies have indicated that when multisensory methods are used there is usually evidence that students' skills and retention rates increase (Cook, 2011; Farkas, 2003; Riggs, 2008).

Multisensory teaching has been advocated and practised for many years, for developing both word recognition and spelling skills (Phillips and Feng, 2012). The approach is often referred to as VAKT (visual-auditory-kinaesthetic-tactile). The tactile component is involved, for example, when young children (or those with a disability) trace a finger over a letter or word that has been made from fuzzy-felt, or cut out from embossed wallpaper. It is believed that the *texture* aids assimilation and recall of the letter shape.

Simultaneous Oral Spelling (SOS)

The self-help strategy called SOS was first developed by Gillingham and Stillman (1960) as part of a multisensory approach to reading and spelling. Note that in applying SOS the *letter name* is used, not its common sound. This makes the method particularly appropriate for older students who may be embarrassed by 'sounding out' words using phonics during tutorials. The approach involves five steps.

- Teacher or tutor selects the target word and pronounces it clearly.
- Student pronounces the word clearly while looking at it in print.
- Student says each syllable in the word, or can break a single-syllable word into initial sound (onset) final sound (rime) (e.g., stop—/st/–/op/).
- Student *names* the letters in the word twice.

- Without reference to the model, the student writes the word while again naming each letter.
- Check, and correct if necessary.

SOS is reported to be an effective intervention strategy and over the years it has been applied very successfully for remediation of spelling problems across a wide age range, including adults (Carreker and Birsh, 2011; Morris and Smith, 2011; Prior, Frye and Fletcher, 1987).

Exaggerated Pronunciation (Over Articulation)

This simple but effective strategy simply requires the teacher and the student to pronounce a tricky word by saying it in the way that it is actually written—climB; WedNESday; acTION; FebRUary; valuABLE; independENT; sepArate; mathEmatics)—stressing the tricky part loudly. The student can even copy and practice writing the word in the way it is printed here. This strategy can be thought of as one form of visual and verbal mnemonic.

Hilte and Reitsma (2006) studied exaggerated pronunciation to facilitate learning of irregular words. Results revealed that the percentage of words spelled correctly substantially increased as a result of training; and memory for the spellings tended to be maintained later. Similarly, Toutanova and Moore (2002) reported that by modelling exaggerated pronunciation they achieved a substantial performance improvement in spelling correction.

Creating a mnemonic

As described in Chapter 5, creating a mnemonic is one strategy that many individuals adopt to help them recall a particularly difficult spelling. The common form of mnemonic uses the correct sequence of letters to create an easy-to-remember phrase: for example, 'laugh'—Long And Ugly Goat Hair; 'choir'—Church Hall Or In Rectory? Nordquist (2011) says that 'the sillier they are the better'.

Mnemonics need not be purely verbal, but can also be made visual (for example, by superimposing a symbol or picture over the word to help recall its pronunciation and letter sequence). This also appears to be appropriate in young children for helping to build up letter recognition and a sight vocabulary of easy words (Shmidman and Ehri, 2010).

There is not much research evidence available to support or refute the value of mnemonics; most of the support comes from anecdotal reports from individuals who say that devising a personal mnemonic helped them overcome a particular spelling demon. Research evidence that does exist suggests that mnemonics can be of value to individuals who are extremely weak spellers, and that it is worth encouraging them in the use of this strategy (Johnson and Obi, 1993).

Old Way/New Way

Old Way/New Way is useful in contexts where a writer habitually misspells certain words and the errors have become firmly established. The strategy was devised by

Lyndon (1989) who identified 'proactive inhibition' as the probable reason for failure of many remedial teaching methods to help a student 'unlearn' incorrect responses. Proactive inhibition describes the situation where previously stored information interferes with a learner's ability to acquire a new response. In other words, what the individual already knows, even erroneous information, is protected from change.

Old Way/New Way uses a student's habitual error as the starting point for change. A memory of the old (incorrect) way of spelling of the word is used to activate an awareness of the new (correct) way of spelling the word. The approach has been found to be reasonably effective (Fisher *et al.*, 2007). The following steps and procedures are used in Old Way/New Way.

- Student writes the word in the usual (incorrect) form.
- Teacher and student agree to call this the 'old way' of spelling that word.
- Teacher shows student a 'new way' (correct way) of spelling the word.
- Attention is drawn to the similarities and differences between the old and the new forms.
- Student writes word again in the old way.
- Student immediately writes word in the new way, and states clearly the differences ('I used to write it as *thay*, but now I know it is *they... thEy... t–h–e–y*').
- Repeat five such writings of old way/new way, and the clear statement of differences.
- Write the word the new way six times, using different colour pens or in different styles. Older students may be asked to write six different sentences using the word in its 'new' form.
- Revise the word or words taught after a two-week interval.
- If necessary, repeat this procedure every two weeks until the new response is firmly established.

Learning regular words

As stated above, 'regular' words are those in which every letter or letter cluster consistently represents a common sound. Obviously, these words are much easier to learn and remember.

Phonetic strategy

In contrast to the visual approach, the phonetic approach stresses the value of attending closely to the sounds within spoken words and then using knowledge of letter-to-sound relationships to encode the words. This is the most effective strategy for learning and writing words that have regular spelling. Teaching the phonetic strategy provides students with a system that can transfer readily to their everyday writing needs, and the system can be used independently by any learner when attempting to spell an unfamiliar word (Amtmann, Abbott and Berninger, 2008).

Research evidence continues to accumulate in full support of using a phonetic approach. For example, Johnston, McGeown and Watson (2012) report that teaching synthetic phonics (in which students are taught to blend sounds) has a positive effect on young children's spelling ability. Similarly, Weiser and Mathes (2011) report clear evidence that systematic instruction in phonic decoding has positive impact on both phonemic awareness and spelling. They argue that such instruction is essential for beginners, and for older learners with literacy difficulties. Increasingly, the importance of providing young children with phonological awareness training is recognized as paving the way for later reading and spelling proficiency (Callaghan and Madelaine, 2012; Duff, Hayiou-Thomas and Hulme, 2012; Robbins and Kenny, 2007; Robinson, 2010).

Traditionally, the classroom study of 'phonics' and 'word families' as a supplement to reading and writing helped young children acquire a good working knowledge of letter-to-sound correspondences. This knowledge was often revealed in the quality of their invented spelling. It is extremely unfortunate that systematic study of phonics and word families was often regarded by whole-language teachers as 'teaching out of context'; so it fell out of favour for two decades. More recently, the importance of including such teaching in every literacy programme has been acknowledged (Rose, 2009).

Analysing words into their component sound units is clearly an important part of the phonetic strategy, and the words used for analysis need to be appropriate for the students' age and ability. For example, very young children should not be expected to segment and blend words that are complex and outside their listening vocabulary (Werfel and Schuele, 2012).

Murray and Steinen (2011) acknowledge the importance of identifying sound units within words, and have devised a system they call '*Word-Map-ping*'. It teaches children to break spoken words into their component sound units *before* looking at the spelling pattern in print. The children then map the sound units to the relevant letters and groups of letters. Murray and Steinen state that the approach '...can be a useful technique for directing spelling study across a wide range of grade levels in general classrooms, in instruction with readers with learning disabilities, and in remedial work with small groups or in tutorials [...] it is well suited for special education students who thrive on direct teaching and close guidance' (p.299).

An intervention using 'sounding out' with somewhat older students in primary and secondary school is *Fonetik Spelling* (Jackson, 2012). This approach capitalizes on phonic decoding to enable very weak spellers to write a reasonable phonic alternative for a word, before checking and correcting it with a handheld Franklin Spell-checker. The approach can be seen demonstrated clearly in a video online at http://ezispel. co.nz/index.htm

Many of the strategies described above can be incorporated in the word study approaches described fully in the next chapter. Word study also enables teachers to expose their upper primary and secondary students to morphology and etymology as part of their vocabulary development. In the new National Curriculum in the UK, it is expected that children at the end of Year 5–6 level should begin to use knowledge of morphology and etymology to guide their own spelling.

Best practices

- It is essential to teach all students a range of self-help strategies for spelling regular and irregular words.
- The following strategies all have research data to support their use for learning to spell irregular words: Look-Say-Cover-Write-Check (visual imagery), Simultaneous

Oral Spelling, Exaggerated Pronunciation, Multisensory Approach, and Old Way/ New Way.
- Phonetic spelling has research evidence to support its value for encoding and checking regular words.
- Visual strategies should be taught alongside phonetic strategies to ensure that students can use both strategies in a coordinated and complementary manner.

Online and print resources

- *Effective Spelling Strategies* (2013). Item available on All About Learning Press website at: http://www.allaboutlearningpress.com/effective-spelling-strategies
- A useful online interactive programme using LCWC principles can be found at: http://www.ictgames.com/lcwc.html. It is geared to the early primary school years, but is also relevant for older poor spellers.
- Beating Dyslexia.com website has an item titled *Spelling help: How to spell any word*. http://www.beatingdyslexia.com/spelling-help.html
- A PowerPoint presentation on spelling strategies can be located at: http://www. slideshare.net/joannerudling/slideshare-spelling-strategies-memory-tricks
- *Spelling strategies*. An online document with practical advice at: http://www.csu. edu.au/__data/assets/pdf_file/0004/82768/strategiesandapostrophes.pdf
- *English: Word level: Spelling strategies*. Available online at: http://www.primary resources.co.uk/english/englishA3e.htm#strategies
- Morris, H. and Smith, S. (2011). *33 ways to help with spelling*. London: Fulton.

Chapter 7

Word study

It is only in fairly recent years that educators and researchers have recognized fully the importance of including the study of words as part of any high quality literacy programme (Davis, 2013; Fountas and Pinnell, 2004; Joseph and Orlins, 2005; Rasinski and Zutell, 2010; Scott, 2010; Scraper, 2002). Word study is now regarded as a 'best practice' for combining spelling instruction and vocabulary enhancement. Word study, according to Leipzig (2000), is an alternative to traditional approaches to teaching spelling. This mainly *morphemic approach* helps students understand how words are constructed, and how and why some words share common groups of letters and obey certain rules.

Templeton and Morris (2001) advise that beyond instruction in spelling patterns, teaching should begin to emphasize word study as part of language development in a broader sense. They suggest that as students get older the teaching should stress the interrelatedness of spelling, phonics, morphology, etymology and vocabulary. The research conducted to date suggests that word study can significantly advance students' spelling skills (Abbott, 2001; Cook, 2003; Crouse and Landers, 2011; Hutcheon, Campbell and Stewart, 2012; Joseph and Orlins, 2005; Kingsley, 2012).

The what, how and why of word study

The term 'word study' covers a wide range of activities of varying degrees of complexity (Dew, 2012; Newingham, 2010). Beginning in the early school years, by studying words from a purely phonological perspective (how to detect and represent sounds and syllables within spoken words), word study should gradually extend over the later primary school years to include a deeper understanding of structure and morphemic features (root words, prefixes, suffixes) and the principles that apply when these morphemic elements are combined (Devonshire, Morris and Fluck, 2013). It is not until the secondary school years that teaching could also focus on interesting etymological aspects of words—although some reference to interesting word origins can occur earlier if it is relevant to a given curriculum topic.

In terms of the 'what' and 'how' aspects of word study, a paper by Louisa Moats (2005) provides an excellent framework for dealing with the study of words across the primary (elementary) school years. The principles and content covered at any age level should be appropriate for the learners' developmental level in spelling skills (Davis, 2013; Scott, 2010).

For the youngest children in kindergarten, word study is mainly related to helping them develop awareness of the separate sounds within spoken words (phoneme awareness), and how these sounds can be represented by letters. This basic knowledge helps them, for example, to spell simple words (e.g. *dog, set, Mum, Dad, bag, sit*), and some may begin to understand consonant digraphs such as /ch/ (*chop; chin; chat*) and consonant blends such as /tr/ (*trot; tree; trap*). At this stage they should also become proficient in splitting single-syllable words into onset and rime units (in the word *trot*, /tr/ is the onset, and /ot/ is the rime). As children progress through the primary school years this very basic knowledge is extended to include attention to syllables, compound words, and morphemic elements such as root words, prefixes and suffixes. For example, children need to understand that suffixes can signify plurality (book; book*s*), verb tense (walk*ed*; walk*ing*), or comparative or superlative forms of adjectives (small*er*, small*est*).

Watson (2013) has stated that word study makes an important contribution to learning to spell because it helps students recognize connections between words, and how change in meaning can influence the spelling of a particular word (e.g., *construct* can become *construction*; *inform* can become *informed, informing, information*). Through the medium of word study primary school children can more easily recognize that an unfamiliar word such as *selfishly* is simply a derivative of a very familiar word they can already spell (*self*) and is not written as *sellfishlee*. Davis (2013, p.3) suggests that: 'Word study enables children to examine the complete orthographic makeup of words and word parts and helps to cement visual recognition and memory of the appropriate letter strings.'

In terms of 'what' to use for word study material, any online search using the term 'word study' will yield an abundant supply of activities and programmes from which teachers can select material according to the current abilities and needs of their students. However, it must be noted that some resources online appear to be almost random collections of word exercises, puzzles and games, not sequenced or organized in a way that reflects any understanding of developmental progression in spelling strategy development. The same criticism can be levelled at many published books containing 'spelling exercises'. Most of these activities do no harm, but they may not really advance a child's abilities or increase genuine interest in words. Some word puzzles, such as word-search and crosswords, tend to be too easy for students who are already competent spellers, but frustrating for weak spellers. Any incidental learning that occurs when completing such 'busywork' is unlikely to transfer to children's everyday writing and spelling.

Some of the most useful word study activities include Word Sorts and word families (Bear *et al.*, 2012; Ganske, 2006, 2008; Johnston, 1999; Leipzig, 2000; Newingham, 2010; Scraper, 2002). These two activities can be used separately, or can be integrated as a way of extending children's learning of orthographic principles.

Word Sorts

Word Sorts represent an investigative approach to helping students identify orthographic features within and across words. Davis (2013, p.4) explains: 'By comparing, contrasting and classifying patterns within words, students reinforce concepts about how words work, their structure, letter sequences and how these inform both sound and meaning.' Comparing and contrasting words in this way helps students discover and appreciate important orthographic principles. In turn, this understanding aids both spelling and word recognition, because students retain clear mental images of root words and morphemes (Apel, 2007). An example of a Word Sort is presented later, in Appendix 8.

A study by Cook (2003), with students aged 9 to 12 years, suggests that word sorting pitched at students' developmental level improves memory and generalization of spelling patterns, and results in consistently higher test scores when compared to traditional teaching and testing methods. A similar result was obtained by Rook (2012) with Grade 4 students from three states in the US.

It is important to begin with easy material with which students can quickly experience high levels of success. A typical Word Sort activity involves giving students a set of word cards containing a group of words to be compared. For a simple example, the words might be: *sock, black, truck, lock, rack, luck, trick, track, block, lick, sack, stick, flock, flick,* and *suck.* The students are asked, 'What is the same about these words?' The response might be that the words all end with /ck/. The words might now be categorized in other ways by sorting the cards into groups—for example, words ending in /ock/; words ending in /ack/; words beginning with a digraph or consonant blend.

At a more advanced level, Word Sorts can involve words that are grouped according to the meaning and spelling connection—for example, *played, playfully, replay, player, playground, horseplay.* Or the words supplied may be of this type: *real, realist, realistic, reality, realism, unreal*; *fantasy, fantastic, fantastical, heal, healthy, healer, healthful, healthiness.*

Alternatively the set of words may focus on the meaning of a particular morpheme (e.g., the suffix –*ity*): *fatality, neutrality, nationality, reality, ability, sincerity.* Morphemes are important because their spelling is consistent across all words that contain them.

Word Sorts provide opportunities for students to be taught (or to discover) the connections that exist among words; and students can recognize the most basic of spelling rules. Leipzig (2000, p.106) states: 'To implement word study effectively, teachers and students alike must become word detectives, engaged in an ongoing attempt to make sense of word patterns and their relationships to one another.'

Findings from research into the effects of using Word Sorts (e.g., Joseph and Orlins, 2005; Rasinski and Zutell, 2010; Scraper, 2002) indicate that:

- requiring students to compare words by their root words, and to manipulate prefixes and suffixes, teaches these important elements in effective and meaningful ways;
- beyond the benefits to spelling, Word Sorts also help older students increase their vocabulary and word recognition skills;
- the experiences involved in Word Sorts are particularly helpful to students with learning difficulties, and also to students learning English as a second language;
- Word Sorts can be used with a whole class, groups, or individuals;
- parents can easily understand the purpose of the activity and can help their children engage with it for homework.

To this list of benefits, we can add outcomes from a study by Crouse and Landers (2011) involving students in Grade 1. They suggest that:

- children who actively participate in Word Sorts show growth in both reading and spelling;
- it is necessary to differentiate the difficulty level of Word Sorts, based on children's current instructional level and special needs;
- Word Sorts can help children discover and use spelling features that they have not yet been taught.

Directed Spelling Thinking Activity (DSTA)

DSTA is a form of Word Sort that can involve a group of students in comparing, contrasting and categorizing a set of words based on points of similarity or differences (Zutell, 1996). The aim is to help students attend to spelling patterns, rhyme, and phonic predictability. For example, the students may explore the words *pail, pale, fail, male, mail, kale, sail, sale, rail, retail, entail, snail, tale,* and discover that the long /a/ sound can be represented by two different letter clusters. They then study other sets of words to identify any containing these letter clusters, and identify any other letter or letter combinations that represent the long /a/ sound (for example, some words containing –*ay: pay, lay, today*…).

Over a period of time, classroom lists of words that illustrate a particular letter group, rhyming words, a spelling rule, or multiple derivations from a root word can be constructed and used as a reference point, and for regular revision and practice (Hutcheon, Campbell and Stewart, 2012). This type of word study activity has been particularly recommended for older students with specific learning difficulties in the literacy domain (Graham, Harris and Loynachan, 1996).

Word families

Word families are groups of words that share common visual, phonologic or morphemic features. Basal spelling programmes usually contain many such groupings of words— underpinned by the belief that working with these word families helps children learn important letter sequences that commonly occur. Davis (2013) states that word families help to establish an awareness of spelling structures and letter sequences that can generalize to the spelling of thousands of other words.

Studying a specific word family usually involves reading the words aloud, noting similarities and differences, underlining or colour-coding the important letter string, writing the words from memory, and using the words in sentences. It is common practice then to display a large-print version of the word family on a wall-chart in the classroom, so that it can be revisited occasionally and, most importantly, can serve as a reference when children are engaged in writing.

Here is an example of a small word family for establishing the letter string /ean/ as a rhyme and a mental orthographic image:

bean,
   lean
      mean
         clean
I mean, this bean is lean and clean!

Based on children's age and level of spelling development, teachers would need to decide whether to include the less common words *dean, glean, wean*.

Having read and studied the /ean/ words teachers might, on a different day, ask: 'Can we add *–ing* to any of these words and still make a real word?' 'Can we add *–ed*?' 'Can we add *–est*?' On another occasion, the teacher might include this group of words within a Word Sort, together with the words *keen, preen, scene, screen, been, teen,* so that the students can learn that other letter groups can also be used to represent the sound unit /ean/.

Word Walls

Beginning in kindergarten and extending throughout the primary school years, the practice of displaying new words on charts and flashcards on the classroom wall is one way of arousing children's interest. At the same time these words then provide a resource that children can instantly refer to when writing. Watson (2013) suggests that Word Walls provide a great strategy for young learners to see and write the words they need, when they need them. Although initially the words on a particular chart may be topic related, and written in random order, later it helps if the Word Wall words can be reorganized in alphabetical order, to serve as an easier point of reference when writing.

Material on a Word Wall may include high-frequency words, word families, thematic words, 'words of the week', and 'common spelling demons'. Gursky (2003) suggests that a Word Wall is a tool to be used, not just a display. Students should be encouraged to add material to the wall, and to use it for word games and activities, as well as for writing purposes.

Teachers' professional knowledge

Scott (2010, p.4) says: 'A teacher's knowledge of the structure of English is an important factor in optimizing word study instruction; equally vital is the ability to present the study of spelling, vocabulary and word choice in a manner that engages students and entices them to explore words on a deeper level.'

Unfortunately, several studies have found that teachers' own depth of knowledge of spelling principles and morphology is often extremely lacking (Fielding-Barnsley, 2010; Goldfus, 2012; Henry, 2010; Marszalek, 2012; Meehan and Hammond, 2006; Washburn, Joshi and Cantrell, 2011). This is largely due to the fact that word study, morphology and etymology are not included in the curriculum of trainee teachers today, even for those majoring in English. For this reason, it is difficult for teachers to become enthusiastic about a topic on which they feel they have limited knowledge.

One important step that any teacher can take is to arouse their own interest in words by appropriate study. An excellent starting point would be David Crystal's entertaining, wonderfully readable, and highly informative book *The story of English in 100 words* (2011). If, for example, you wonder why there is a 'b' in *debt,* or a 'p' in *receipt*, Crystal will explain. Another book that contains a wealth of information on vocabulary and etymology is *Word power made easy* (Lewis, 1978). This is an older text, but the information presented therein has not dated in the least.

It is also easy for teachers to find out more about words, and how to help children explore them, by conducting online searches using terms such as 'word study' and 'word families'. Other suggestions can be found in the resources listed at the end of this chapter.

Best practices

- The teaching of spelling must help students gain a better understanding of how words are constructed and reconstructed to convey precise meanings.
- Word study activities geared to students' stages of development have been shown to increase students' interest in words, and to have benefits for their spelling ability.
- Word study is not an alternative way of approaching spelling. It is simply one important component within a total language programme that also includes explicit instruction, frequent writing, and corrective feedback.

Online and print resources

- Ganske, K. (2000). *Word journeys: Assessment-guided phonics, spelling, and vocabulary instruction.* New York: Guilford Press.
- Bear, D.R., Invernizzi, M., Templeton, S. and Johnson, F. (2012). *Words their way: Word study for phonics, vocabulary, and spelling instruction* (5th ed.). Englewood Cliffs, NJ: Pearson-Prentice-Hall.
- Draper, D. (2008). *Thinking spelling.* An extremely valuable resource for teachers—particularly those who feel that their own professional knowledge on word study principles and content is lacking. Available online at: http://www. decd.sa.gov.au/barossa/files/links/thinkingspelling.pdf
- A very useful article on word study by Newingham (2010) provides teaching advice with many practical examples. Available online at the Scholastic website: http://www.scholastic.com/teachers/top_teaching/2010/10/my-november-top-ten-list-word-study-in-action
- Teachers will find of interest the visual material on word families and Word Walls at the Pinterest website: http://pinterest.com/tw5078/word-families/
- Word Walls are clearly discussed and illustrated on The School Bell website at: http://www.theschoolbell.com/Links/word_walls/words.html
- *Directed Spelling Thinking Activity (DSTA).* Available online at: http://www. docstoc.com/docs/40065802/Directed-Spelling-Thinking-Activity-_DSTA_
- The book *Teaching kids to read* contains some very valuable and well-structured word and phonogram lists that teachers and tutors can use for curriculum content. Tran, F. (2010). *Teaching kids to read.* Albert Park, Victoria, Australia: Wilkins Farago.

Chapter 8

Informal methods of assessing spelling

Accurate assessment of students' spelling provides the detailed information to guide teachers in their planning of lessons at group and individual levels. For example, regular assessment helps confirm that all students are mastering a core of high-frequency words needed for daily writing, and are also learning the correct spelling of words related to new curriculum topics taught each week. In particular, assessment can help identify those students who are having major difficulties developing effective spelling skills, so that appropriate interventions can be introduced. Regular assessment of students' spelling can certainly be regarded as best practice.

Classroom assessments

Classroom assessment commonly involves a suitable combination of measures—for example, observing students as they write, inspecting completed written assignments (work samples), formal and informal testing, and discussion with individual students to discover more about the strategies they use and their degree of confidence when spelling (Westwood, 2005).

In the case of students with learning difficulties, assessment may also involve diagnostic procedures to help identify the specific problems they are having. As Moats (2010, p.1) points out:

> When testing students' spelling, it's important to go beyond simply marking words right or wrong. The assessment should be an opportunity to evaluate students' understanding of sounds and conventional spelling patterns. The kinds of words that students miss, and the types of errors they make, are important in evaluating their spelling achievement and their understanding of language structures.

Observing students and evaluating their written work

The most useful way of assessing students' spelling ability is to observe them as they write (Lipson and Wixson, 2012; Ott, 2007). Watching children in action, and discussing their strategies with them after they have finished their work, can reveal much about their level of confidence, the types of errors they tend to make, and their ability to monitor and correct their own errors. For example, a teacher may note whether individual students are willing to take risks with words they use, or are hesitant and tend to restrict themselves only to words they are sure they can spell correctly. Even gifted students can sometimes hide a talent for writing if excessive 'perfectionism' causes them to be unreasonably fearful of making errors in their spelling (Callard-Szulgit, 2012).

Observing a student as he or she writes can help teachers obtain answers to the following important questions:

- What strategies does the student call upon when faced with spelling difficult words?
- Does the student automatically make use of available words on the Word Wall, vocabulary lists, and other resources around the classroom?
- Does the student write quickly and easily, or are handwriting and spelling laborious and time consuming acts?
- When asked to check through the written work, is the student aware of any spelling errors he or she has made?
- Can they self-correct?
- If a student is working with a word processor, how does he or she respond to the immediate feedback provided by the spell-checker?

Information gathered by observation needs to be supplemented by more detailed and specific data obtained from evaluating students' unaided written work. Using these work samples has an advantage over typical spelling tests, because the samples provide a larger corpus of material within which to detect any habitual errors. Habitual errors are obviously more important to locate than chance errors, because they are often very difficult to remedy ('old habits die hard') (Fisher *et al.*, 2007; Lyndon, 1989).

By carefully examining the words that students can spell correctly, as well as any spelling errors they have made, it is possible to gain some insights into the stage of development each student has reached. It is also often possible to recognize the cognitive strategies they seem to be relying on when spelling difficult words. Work samples from a whole class can sometimes highlight a need to provide specific teaching (or re-teaching) of a spelling principle or strategy to all students.

Developmental considerations

The ability to spell words accurately does not *suddenly* emerge, even when teaching methods and opportunities are optimum. The acquisition of any cognitive skill is always a gradual process, with each stage of development reflecting new insights the individual has gained from experience, instruction, practice and feedback (Fresch and Wheaton, 2002). In order to provide the best available instruction in spelling, it is essential that teachers determine the stage of development that each individual student has reached (Sipe, 2008). This is particularly necessary in the case of students who have learning difficulties and who require accurately targeted intervention. At various points in this book readers have been reminded to assess students' stage of development in order to provide teaching and resources that appropriately match the stage. In order to do this, teachers must be aware of the knowledge and strategies typical of each developmental stage.

Children pass through at least four recognizable stages (some experts say five stages) on their way to becoming skilled spellers. They progress through the stages at different rates, and it is unrealistic to expect any student to demonstrate a level of independence and accuracy in spelling that is beyond his or her current developmental level (Manning and Underbakke, 2005).

The brief summary of stages described below is adapted from several sources including Ehri and Wilce (1985), Henderson and Beers (1980), Nunes, Bryant and Bindman (1997), Tompkins (2010b), and Westwood (2011).

Stage 1: Prephonetic (also referred to as 'precommunicative' stage)

At this stage, which is typical of children aged three to five years, a child 'plays' at producing writing in imitation of the writing of others, using a random mix of capital letters and shapes. There is no connection between these scribbles and speech sounds or real words.

Stage 2: Phonetic

At this stage, which typically emerges at age six years, the child relies mainly upon phonemic awareness and a beginning knowledge of letter-to-sound correspondences. Even without instruction, the words children invent at this stage are often quite recognizable, because they are applying aspects of the alphabetic code that they have acquired incidentally. Naturally, many inaccuracies exist at this stage because the spelling of many English words is not entirely predictable. Toward the end of this phonetic stage, the approximations move much nearer to regular letter-to-sound correspondences.

It should be noted that the majority of older individuals with poor spelling have reached this phonetic stage but have not progressed beyond it. Their problem is a tendency to be over-dependent on phonic information, and therefore they write all words as if they have perfect letter-to-sound correspondence. They need to develop more effective ways of processing and remembering words visually in order to build up a store of correct orthographic images.

Stage 3: Transitional

At approximately seven to eight years old children reach a stage where there is clear evidence of a more sophisticated understanding of word structure. The child becomes aware of within-word letter strings and syllable junctures, and is better able to use memory for word images to check what has been written. The children who gain real mastery over spelling at this stage also begin to use words they know already in order to spell words they have never written before (spelling by analogy).

Stage 4: Independence

This stage is achieved by eight plus years in normally developing children, but much later in students with learning difficulties. At this stage children have mastery of quite complex phonic principles and strategies, and use visual imagery effectively when writing and checking familiar words. But even at this stage, spellers still make some errors. Independent spellers are good at self-monitoring and make flexible use of a wide range of spelling, proofreading, and self-correcting strategies.

As indicated above, students with learning difficulties are likely to reach each stage later than their age peers. Some of these students may even reach a plateau in their spelling development unless given help to acquire the knowledge and skill necessary to progress to the next level. Best practice involves taking into account students' stages of development when guiding them along the path to independence.

Classroom testing

During the two decades when whole-language philosophy prevailed in literacy teaching it became popular to criticize the use of spelling tests. They were regarded as a decontextualized and 'unnatural' way of evaluating children's language development. Times change, and it is now generally agreed once again that tests can add considerably to the pool of information that teachers glean from classroom observation and from work samples.

Traditionally, classroom assessment of spelling had usually taken three forms: weekly *classroom testing* of a word list that had been set for students to learn (an informal type of *criterion referenced test*); occasional *standardized* (norm-referenced) *testing* to determine a student's 'spelling age' or spelling quotient, mainly for reporting and record-keeping purposes (as discussed in the next chapter); and *diagnostic testing*, often conducted by a remedial support teacher to help determine the precise instructional needs of students with spelling difficulties.

Before the 1970s, it was always part of a systematic approach to spelling to have a classroom test on Friday each week, based on a set of words given to the students on Monday. In the hands of an efficient teacher, the test results could identify those children who had not reached a criterion of at least eight words correct out of ten, and who could then be provided with additional help to learn the words. The most effective teachers usually differentiated this learning task by having several different lists of words, geared to varying developmental levels of the students. Some teachers also adopted a pre-test/post-test approach, so that students could focus their attention on words they did not already know. Unfortunately, less effective teachers simply marked the test (or asked the children to exchange papers and mark the words themselves). The numerical results were then entered in the teacher's record book, but no form of personalized intervention occurred for those who did not manage to learn the list. Less effective teachers also failed to provide adequate revision of words that had been studied in previous weeks, so students tended not to remember them or use them correctly in their writing (Loeffler, 2005; Stirling, 2011b).

If the weaknesses highlighted above can be avoided, and the words set each week are matched to students' needs and performance levels, then regular assessment of children's spelling actually serves a very valuable purpose. Best practice must include regular classroom testing of students' spelling ability in order to guide instruction. Despite the current trend to abolish the weekly test in many US elementary schools, Gentry (2011, p.2) demands that schools should:

> Bring spelling tests back. Give students weekly pretests and posttests to determine what words and patterns need to be learned; differentiate for above-, on- and below-grade-level; measure instructional outcomes; support your spelling program with new technology that allows for word sorting but only when needed; and put students on a course that leads to less humiliation and more success.

Diagnostic testing and error analysis

Diagnostic assessment usually involves careful inspection of the errors a student with learning difficulties makes in daily writing and under test conditions. This *error analysis* represents a qualitative approach to examining students' mistakes to reveal what the student needs to be taught next in order to become a better speller (Bissaker and Westwood, 2006; Joshi and Aaron, 2005; Wasowicz, 2007).

As part of the diagnostic procedure, separate lists of regular and irregular words are sometimes dictated in order to check a student's ability to tackle both forms. Analysis typically involves discovering whether he or she is relying too much or too little on phonic clues when writing the word. Error analysis may also reveal, for example, that a student tends to add an 'e' to the end of words where it is not required (traine; trame), or may omit the 'e' from the end of many words where it is required (danc; mous), or may omit a letter from a word if the sound it represents is difficult to detect (rige for *ridge*; det for *debt*; nif for *knife*). Another student may have difficulty knowing when to double the consonants when adding 'ing' (shoping; siting). Specific information at this level can lead the teacher to devise relevant and well-targeted word study activities to help overcome the problem.

Error analysis can also reveal more about the stage of development a given student has reached. For example, Joshi and Aaron (2005) suggest that the following errors made by a Grade 4 girl suggested that she is in the transitional stage but not yet fully independent. She wrote dought for *doubt*; vally for *valley*; gramar for *grammar,* and several other words that were incorrect by only one letter. This can be contrasted with a Grade 3 student at the beginning of the phonetic stage of spelling who wrote *cents* as ses; *young* as yug; kag for *cage*; gef for *chief*. This student can detect some key sounds within a word but not other sounds. As a follow-up, it would be important to assess this student's auditory discrimination and also his ability to say the target word correctly.

Limitations of error analysis

Having just extolled the virtues of error analysis to help with instruction of students with difficulties, it must be admitted at this point that the process is far from an exact science. Despite the fact that many writers have devised quite complex systems for analysing spelling errors (systems much akin to 'miscue analyses' used in reading diagnosis) in reality the accuracy of such systems is often greatly overestimated. As Dahl *et al.* (2003) have pointed out, it is usually much more helpful to assess a student's range of spelling and self-correcting strategies, rather than focusing on missing or transposed letters in target words.

Some of the material presented in the Appendix can be used for diagnostic purposes. But such diagnosis is only worth doing if it leads to specific interventions to help students make better progress.

Discussing spelling with individual students

In addition to assessing the knowledge and spelling skills that students with learning difficulties exhibit in their daily writing and in tests, it is relevant also to consider affective factors such as students' attitudes toward spelling—do they regard accurate and careful spelling as important? Do they regard themselves as competent and confident in their own ability to spell?

Often the discussion with an individual student can focus on relevant work samples from his or her daily writing, and can involve some degree of self-assessment (Loeffler, 2005). Can the student identify any errors in the work? Can they indicate how they attempt to spell or correct difficult words? What do they do with the corrective feedback they receive from the teacher? Do they find spell-checkers on the computer helpful? What do they feel would help to make them more competent spellers?

Best practices

- Regular assessment of students' spelling skills is essential in order that teaching activities can be tailored to the current needs and abilities of the students.
- The most comprehensive profile of students' knowledge, skills and strategies can be constructed from relevant information gleaned from classroom observation, regular marking of students' written assignments, testing, and talking with individual students about their level of confidence and the strategies they use.
- Error analysis can sometimes help identify the specific difficulties a student may be having, so that intervention can be more accurately targeted.

Online and print resources

- Bear, D.R., Invernizzi, M., Templeton, S. and Johnson, F. (2012). *Words their way: Word study for phonics, vocabulary, and spelling instruction* (5th ed.). Englewood Cliffs, NJ: Pearson-Prentice-Hall.
- Fresch, M.J. and Wheaton, A. (2002). *Teaching and assessing spelling.* New York: Scholastic Professional Books.
- Larsen, S., Hammill, D.D. and Moats, L.C. (2013). *Test of written spelling: 5th Edition* (TWS-5). Austin, TX: ProEd.
- Louisiana Department of Education: *Assessing Developmental Spelling.* Online website providing links to the Monster Test of Developmental Spelling (Gentry). http://sda.doe.louisiana.gov/Lists/Assessment%20Section/DispForm.aspx?ID=11
- McDowe, L., Martins, J., Kmiech, T., Shull, C. and Johnson, M. (2010). Assessing and teaching spelling. Online PowerPoint presentation available at: http://ppt. english6.net/assessing-and-teaching-spelling-university-of-minnesota-duluth-e286.html
- NSW Department of Education and Training (2007). *Writing and spelling strategies: Assisting students who have additional support needs.* A comprehensive coverage of teaching and assessing spelling and writing skills. http://www.schools. nsw.edu.au/media/downloads/schoolsweb/studentsupport/programs/ lrngdificulties/writespell.pdf

Chapter 9

Formal assessment of spelling

In addition to the informal classroom assessment procedures used to guide instructional planning, accurate assessment is also needed for purposes of accountability. This infers that best practice at systemic level involves checking that literacy teaching in schools is resulting in effective learning, and that standards in written language are being maintained or improved. This type of assessment is usually carried out using a combination of standardized tests and survey instruments provided as part of a national curriculum.

Standardized testing

Standardized tests are often used by teachers at the beginning and end of each school year as one method of assessing students' progress objectively. Educational psychologists and support teachers often still use such tests as part of their overall evaluation of a student with learning difficulties. Standardized tests are also often used as pre- and post-test measures in research projects designed to evaluate gains from intervention programmes.

Standardized spelling tests are instruments that have been carefully designed and administered to a large representative population of students at various ages. From data collected during the standardization process 'age norms' were calculated, reflecting the typical score (and spread of scores) obtained by students at each age level. This score is often referred to as a 'spelling age'—for example, an eleven-year-old student who is a weak speller might score a spelling age equivalent to that of an average eight-year-old. Tests scores might also be expressed as spelling quotients, standardized scores, or percentile ranks. It is this type of formal testing that was criticized most harshly by whole-language enthusiasts; but many teachers still regard standardized tests as useful indicators of each student's current level. For many teachers, 'spelling age' remains a meaningful concept.

In the US, standardized spelling subtests are often used from assessment batteries such as the *Iowa Tests of Basic Skills*, *Kaufman Test of Educational Achievement*, *Peabody Individual Achievement Test*, *Test of Written Spelling, Fourth Edition* (TWS-4), or the *Wide Range Achievement Test*. In the UK, the *British Spelling Tests Series* (GL Assessments, 2008) is often used, while schools in Australia and New Zealand usually make use of the *South Australian Spelling Test* (SAST) (Westwood, 2005).

Kohnen, Nickels and Castles (2009) have reviewed a number of available assessment instruments for spelling. They regard two tests to be of excellent value for classroom and remedial purposes—the *Single Word Spelling Test* (Sacre and Masterson, 2000) and the *British Spelling Test Series* (Vincent and Crumpler, 1997).

Standardized tests may take the form of a graded word list that is dictated by the tester while students write their responses. Other formats include dictated passages of text, multiple-choice sets of words with students required to identify the word with the correct spelling in each set, and passages of text containing errors for students to proofread and correct. Studies have shown that these various ways of assessing spelling tend to rank children's spelling performance in the much the same way (Moseley, 1997; Westwood, 1999).

Standardized spelling tests are useful for gaining a general impression of the spread of spelling achievement across a whole class or age cohort, but they are fairly limited as sources of diagnostic information. It is impossible to know whether a particular error is habitual, or simply occurred on that day by chance. The typical standardized test contains too few items to provide an adequate sample from which to determine consistent error patterns; and tests usually do not reveal much about the student's ability to self-monitor and self-correct.

In the US, the use of standardized test scores as the sole criterion to evaluate the relative quality of individual schools has been severely criticized (NCFOT, 2008). Many other variables need to be taken into account when attempting to gauge trends in school achievement and improvement.

National surveys

In recent years, in the name of accountability, there has been an increase in the use of *national surveys* of students' literacy skills. These surveys are designed to maintain regular checks on trends in literacy standards within and across countries. Students' performance is usually rated against a set of age-related standards, and the numbers of students performing at the expected standard, or above or below that standard, are reported to schools and to parents. Examples of these surveys include the *National Assessment Programme: Literacy and Numeracy* (NAPLAN) in Australia (ACARA, 2011b), statewide standards tests in the US (e.g., *California Standards Tests: CSTs*) (California Department of Education, 2009), the *Standard Assessment Tests* (SATs) related to the National Curriculum in Britain (Gov.UK., 2013), and the *National Evaluation and Monitoring Project* (NEMP) in New Zealand (Ministry of Education, NZ: 2013).

As an example, in England all students at end of Key Stage 2 undertake statutory grammar, punctuation and spelling tests. Key Stage 2 equates approximately with ages 7–11 (school years 3, 4, 5 and 6). The words assessed are selected to take account of children's developing ability to spell a wide range of words, including common, polysyllabic words, words that conform to regular patterns and words with irregular patterns. The expectation is that students who have reached this stage should be able to spell words correctly by using their knowledge of regular patterns of spelling, word families, root words, and derivations (including prefixes, suffixes and inflections). The test format at Levels 3–5 in Key Stage 2 involves the test administrator reading aloud 20 words to be inserted by the students into appropriate gaps in target sentences. At Level 6 there are 15 such words chosen to demonstrate additional spelling strategies required for lower-frequency, less familiar words (DFE [UK], 2012b; Standards and Testing Agency [UK], 2012).

Similar standards are specified in Australia. In that country the *National Assessment Programme: Literacy and Numeracy* (NAPLAN) has established 'minimum standards' in spelling for students in school years 3, 5, 7 and 9 (ACARA, 2011b). In the period between 2008, when NAPLAN testing began, and 2012 there has been a gradual increase in the number of students reaching or exceeding the set minimum standard in Years 3 and 5 but not much change detected in Year 7, and no improvement at Year 9 (ACARA, 2012b, 2012c). It is interesting to note much the same phenomenon in the US, with spelling growth reaching a plateau at Grade 7 (Foorman and Petscher, 2010).

In the US, spelling standards are usually specified in each state-level curriculum guidelines. For example, in Arizona children at the end of Grade 3 are expected to:

*   Use conventional spelling for high-frequency and other studied words and for adding suffixes to base words (e.g., *sitting, smiled, cries, happiness*).
*   Use spelling patterns and generalizations (e.g., word families, position-based spellings, syllable patterns, ending rules, meaningful word parts) in writing words.
*   Consult reference materials, including beginning dictionaries, as needed to check and correct spellings (Arizona Department of Education, 2012).

National surveys of literacy skills can help administrators and educators to monitor changes in all students' achievement levels over time. For example, in New Zealand Jackson (2008) reviewed data for writing skills from the NEMP conducted by the University of Otago for 1998, 2002, 2006, 2010. The survey covers assessment of students in Year 4 (age 8–9 years) and Year 8 (age 12–13 years). Jackson concluded that despite some small changes in test scores over the period there had been no really significant improvement in students' spelling, punctuation, grammar since 2002. Boys were considerably weaker than girls in writing skills—a phenomenon also noted in the data produced in the UK (Massey and Dexter, 2002).

Criticisms of national testing

There are criticisms levelled at the format used to assess spelling ability in some national testing programmes (Jackson, 2008; Wigglesworth, Simpson and Loakes, 2011; Willet and Gardiner, 2009). A common format adopted involves multiple-choice items in which only one word is correct (e.g., 1. frute, 2. fruit, 3. friut, 4. froot), or presenting a passage of text with embedded spelling errors for students to proofread and correct. The latter form of test tends to contaminate evaluation of spelling ability by also requiring the simultaneous use of reading skills.

Critics argue that many students perform poorly in multiple-choice and proofreading tests, and that they actually spell more accurately in their everyday writing. Willet and Gardiner (2009), commenting on NAPLAN in Australia, conclude that a dictation task is a better test of orthographic knowledge and allows students to focus their cognitive resources on correctly spelling a single word at a time. The format used currently in the UK tests seems to have addressed this problem to some extent, by requiring students to recall and write words dictated by the tester into appropriate gaps in meaningful target sentences (Standards and Testing Agency [UK], 2012). Examples of this format can be located at the website listed under *Online and print resources*.

Another criticism that could be made of the survey tests used in the UK and Australia is that they contain too few items to provide a really reliable and comprehensive assessment of an individual student's spelling skills. Brief tests, while they may be valid in terms of the content they contain, can still be unreliable in terms of test-retest reliability. In other words, students' scores on the test (or a parallel version of the test) may vary from day to day.

National surveys of literacy are also criticized for allowing the creation of 'league tables', showing the relative standing of different schools. This can have a depressing effect on morale in disadvantaged schools with higher-than-average numbers of students failing to achieve the minimum standard.

Nevertheless, despite these criticisms, national and state-level testing of students' knowledge and skills in spelling does serve a valuable purpose in tracking changes in standards. Individual schools can, for example, set goals to increase the number of students who achieve at or above the expected standards and reduce the number of students with difficulties. The renewed interest in improving the teaching of spelling in our schools can be attributed in large part to the information that such testing has revealed.

Best practices

- Standardized tests and data from national testing programmes are both important sources for monitoring spelling standards over time and across countries.
- Schools should make full use of data from national surveys to improve the spelling achievements of their students.
- Teachers should avoid specific coaching of students on words that are likely to appear in tests. This situation simply inflates students' scores to a higher standard than they would normally reach, and presents an inaccurate picture of their everyday spelling ability.

Online and print resources

- G.A. Troia (Ed.) (2010). *Instruction and assessment for struggling writers: Evidence-based practices*. New York: Guilford Press.
- The SAST is a good example of a norm-referenced standardized test. It provides spelling ages for students in the range 6–16 years, and also identifies students who are in the bottom 10 per cent of their age group. Source: Westwood, P. (2005) *Spelling: Approaches to teaching and assessment* (2nd ed.). Melbourne: Australian Council for Educational Research.
- For a good review of available classroom tests see: Kohnen, S., Nickels, L. and Castles, A. (2009). Assessing spelling skills and strategies: A critique of available resource. *Australian Journal of Learning Difficulties, 14,* 1: 113–150.
- Examples of the test format used for spelling within the national testing programme in the UK can be found at: http://media.education.gov.uk/assets/files/pdf/g/2013-297_mlp_l35_gps_paper2_001.pdf
- Examples of the format used in NAPLAN testing in Australia can be found on the website at: http://www.nap.edu.au/verve/_resources/Example_Test_Language_Conventions_Y3.pdf

Appendix

A.1 High priority early words

At an early stage on the path to writing all children should be helped to learn this core of high-frequency everyday words. Some of the words can be mastered easily using the phonetic approach, but most will need to be stored and remembered by using visual and kinaesthetic strategies such as Cover-Copy-Check and repeated writing (see Chapter 6).

A: a about after all also an and any are as at

B: back be because been being between big boy brother bus but by

C: can can't could

D: Dad did do down

F: father first for friend from

G: get girl go good got

H: had has have he her him his hot how

I: if in into is it its

J: just

K: know

L: like little

M: made make many may me Mum Mama more mother my

N: new no not now

O: of on one only or other our out over

P: people playing

R: ran red run

S: said school see she should so some such

T: than that the their them then there these they think this those three time to two

U: up under

V: very

W: was   way   we   well   went   were   what   when   which   who   will   with   would

Y: years   you   your

Note: The reference book *Oxford guide to plain English* (Cutts, 2009) contains a comprehensive list of the most commonly used nouns, verbs, adjectives and adverbs in written and spoken English, arranged in priority order—an invaluable resources for teachers.

A.2 Common initial consonant digraphs and blends

Automatic recognition of the following phonic units is essential for reading and spelling beyond the very earliest level.

*   A digraph is a cluster of two letters that represent a single speech sound.

    ch   sh   th   wh   qu   ph

A consonant blend is a cluster of letters representing a pronounceable unit in which the sound commonly associated with each letter can still be heard.

br   bl   cr   cl   dr   fr   fl   gr   gl   tr
pr   pl   st   sp   sc   sk   sl   sw   sn   sm

Three letter blends:

str   spl   thr   scr   shr   spr   squ

A.3 Simple word building

The following phonograms can be used to build a large number of new words. Students can be asked to think of as many words as possible that can be constructed from each of these units by adding a single initial letter, or a digraph, or consonant blend. This word-building activity helps to establish and reinforce important orthographic images that are essential components of both word recognition and spelling.

```
–amp  –ump  –and  –end  –ast  –est  –ist
–ust  –ank  –ink  –all  –ill  –ull  –ell
–ant  –ent  –int  –ing  –old  –alk  –ilk
–elt  –ilt  –atch  –itch  –unch  –uch  –act
–ift  –ong  –orm  –orn  –ulk  –umb  –oss
–ar  –ay  –ea  –ate  –ure  –er  –ow
–atch  –eer  –igh  –ight  –ance  –ain  –ang
```

A.4 Diagnostic testing

Phonetically regular spellings

The following words can be used to assess a student's ability to apply phonic knowledge to the spelling of simple words. The list also provides an opportunity to examine the student's knowledge of a selection of consonant blends and digraphs used in the initial and final position.

at   if   on   up   wet
bag   rod   fin   bus   men
chop   plot   ship   trap   step
flag   swim   glad   drop   slug
must   risk   silk   send   lamp
fact   help   sift   luck   song
brag   blog   crab   clap   frog
grab   pram   spot   scan   skim
snag   smack   think   shack   when
scrap   string   split   shred   thrill

Irregular words

ask   are   any   was   they
sure   said   word   come   work
half   bath   wash   blue   birth
knife   does   climb   who   learn
colour   laugh   answer   juice   women
master   lawn   tough   purple   choir

The Freereading.net website contains some large-print flashcards that can be downloaded for teaching and testing irregular words: http://www.freereading.net/index.php?title=Irregular_word_cards

A.5 Words we often misspell

accommodation
achieve
acknowledgment (but see *knowledgeable*)
address
adolescent
all right (two words, not *alright*)
argument
attendance
business
ceiling
committee
conscience

definite
desperate
embarrass
existence
fascination
foreign
government
grammar
interrupt
it's (*it is* or *it has*); its (possessive form)
knowledge
knowledgeable
library
lose (misplace something); loose (not fixed)
maintenance
mathematics
measurable
miniature
necessary
noticeable
parallel
personal (related to a person); personnel (staff, workers)
principal (most important)
privilege
receive
recommend
separate
surprise
temperature
they're (they are)
weird
you're (you are)

A.6 Common prefixes and suffixes

An essential aspect of teaching students about *morphemes* is to draw attention to the way in which prefixes and suffixes influence the meaning of the root word to which they are added. Some examples below serve as a starting point, but there are many other affixes that can be studied. The following website is an excellent source: http://www.prefixsuffix.com/rootchart.php

Prefixes

anti –   meaning 'opposite' or 'against': e.g., anticlimax; antidepressant; antihero
bi –   meaning 'two': e.g., bicycle; binary; bilateral
de–   meaning 'away from' or 'to undo': e.g., detach; depart; deconstruct
inter– meaning 'between': e.g., interrupt; intercede; interval

mis–	meaning 'wrong': e.g., mistake; misconception; misspell
post–	meaning 'behind' or 'after': e.g., post-test; post-mortem; postscript
re–	meaning 'again' or 'repeat': e.g., rewrite; reprint; react
sub–	meaning 'below' or 'under': e.g., submarine; substandard; subhuman
trans–	meaning 'across' or 'beyond': e.g., transport; transfer; transcend

Suffixes

–able or *–ible*	meaning 'capable of': e.g., lovable; edible; notable
–er	signifying 'someone who does': e.g., worker; painter; dressmaker
–ish	used to form adjectives from nouns to convey a tendency toward or characteristic of: e.g., foolish; babyish; reddish
–ist	signifying an 'occupation' or 'connection': e.g., artist; socialist; pianist
–less	meaning 'without' or 'lacking': e.g., faultless; homeless; ageless
–ness	meaning 'the state of being': happiness; loneliness; illness
–ly	meaning 'how' or 'in the manner': swiftly; happily; carefully
–ous	meaning 'characterized by' or 'full of a quality': e.g., rebellious; joyous; nervous
–est	added to adjectives and adverbs to convey the meaning of superlative degree: e.g., warmest; fastest; richest
–logy or *–ology*	meaning 'the study of': e.g., biology; cardiology; geology

A.7 Some rules worth remembering

As explained in Chapter 5, it is not recommended that the classroom spelling programme be entirely based on teaching and drilling rules. Many spelling rules are far too complex for the average student to understand, remember and apply. And almost all rules have too many exceptions to make them of much value. *However*, as part of word study activities with upper primary and secondary students, it can sometimes be useful to discuss rules, and to encourage them to discover words that do, or do not, conform to a given rule.

- **I before E.** Examples: *believe; relieve; retrieve; piece; thief; friend.* Exceptions: *caffeine; eight; foreign; either; height; leisure; neither; protein; seized; weight; weird.* **Except after C.** Examples: *deceive; perceive; receive; ceiling.* Exceptions: *ancient; efficient; science; society; sufficient.*
- **Silent 'e' rule.** The final 'e' on the end of a word usually causes the first vowel in the word to be pronounced with its long sound (its name). A very large family of words obeys this rule. Examples: *date; tale; cite; dose; hide; crude.* Exceptions to the rule include: *done; have; lose.*
- **Drop the final 'e' on a root word before adding a suffix that begins with a vowel, but not before a suffix beginning with a consonant.** Examples: *hide* becomes *hiding; sane* becomes *sanity.* But *like* becomes *likeness; arrange* becomes *arrangement.* Common error: *truly* (not *truely*).

- **Words that end in the letter 'y' must change 'y' to 'i' before adding a suffix.** Examples: *try* becomes *tries* and *tried*; *puppy* becomes *puppies*; *happy* becomes *happiness*; *fury* becomes *furious*; *marry* becomes *marriage*.
- For other rules (and their exceptions) see:
  - Reading from Scratch website at: http://www.dyslexia.org/spelling_rules.shtml
  - Free Home-school Curriculum Spelling Course at: http://www.splashesfromtheriver.com/spelling/spelling_rules.htm
  - The Love To Know website also contains useful information at: http://grammar.yourdictionary.com/spelling-and-word-lists/spelling-rules.html

A.8 Word Sort

Here is one example of a simple Word Sort, suitable for middle primary school children, or for older students with spelling difficulties.

each   itch   catch   hatch   ditch   teach   reach
witch   match   stitch   patch   peach   latch   pitch

1   Sort the words into three groups, and explain your reasons.
2   Take two words from each group and write a sentence to show the meaning of each word.
3   Work with a partner. Take turns to dictate four of the words for your partner to write down and check.
4   Two words in the whole set cannot have the letters 'ing' added to make a real word. Which are the two words?
5   The ending 'ed' cannot be added to some of the words to make a real word? Which words here cannot end in 'ed'?

A.9 Hyphens

Hyphens are used to connect component parts of compound words, and to separate some prefixes from their root words. Their use is always to help convey the precise meaning of a word or phrase, and sometimes to aid pronunciation. Competence in spelling also includes the ability to use hyphens appropriately. *If in doubt, consult a dictionary to check whether or not a specific word requires a hyphen.*

Hyphens are governed by fewer consistent rules than other elements of punctuation and spelling, and their use is open to flexibility and change. Over time, some words that were hyphenated originally tend to drop the hyphen eventually to become unified—for example: e-mail (*email*), to-day (*today*), life-like (*lifelike*), anti-climax (*anticlimax*), hyper-link (*hyperlink*), pre-historic (*prehistoric*), girl-friend (*girlfriend*), pre-service teachers (*preservice*). During the transition, both forms of the word co-exist for a while in written language, and it is left to writers to make their own choices. Recent examples of change in progress are the words *cooperation, coordinate,* and *coordinator.* Increasingly, these words are now written without the hyphen; but many authors still continue to use *co-operation, co-ordinate,* and *co-ordinator.* In general, the current trend is to do away with hyphens when possible.

While many words with prefixes do not require a hyphen (e.g., *antibiotic, bifocal, disorder, extramarital, hyperactivity, nonstop, oncoming, overstate, preamble, reform, semiconscious, subheading, triangular*, and hundreds of other examples), some words containing prefixes do need hyphens. For example, *co-wrote, co-existing, bi-monthly, de-emphasize, ex-president, ex-boyfriend, in-built, all-important*. Similarly hyphens appear within some compound words: *sugar-free, trade-in, make-up*, but not in *takeover, twofold, lifeless, blackout, wavelike*. The most recent advice in the APA Style Manual is to write most words formed with prefixes and suffixes as one word.

Often the hyphen is introduced to avoid several letters coming together in a form that interrupts the easy visual perception and pronunciation of the word, for example, words such as these do need a hyphen: *antiinflammatory, coownership, preeminent, coworker, deice* (de-ice), *semiindependent, metaanalysis*. These are examples of what is referred to as 'letter collisions'. The hyphen helps with visual processing, pronunciation and spelling.

When a compound word (a compound modifier) serves as an adjective to modify a noun, the component words are usually hyphenated to make the meaning crystal clear. For example, a *long-term* relationship; a *devil-may-care* attitude; a *six-year-old* student; a *deep-water* trawler; a *short-sighted* professor; a *quick-thinking* robber; a *camera-ready* diagram, an *all-too-common* opinion, an *out-of-date* magazine. [Contrast these with 'a man eating alligator'. Is this an alligator that eats men, or a man who is currently eating an alligator? A *man-eating alligator* makes the meaning clear!]

The current convention is not to employ a hyphen if an adverb ends in 'ly', for example, we should NOT write a *carefully-executed* dive, *a rapidly-changing* background, a *thoughtfully-structured* response. These should be written without the hyphens. Nor should we hyphenate words where an adjective is coupled with the infinitive verb form ('to'), for example, *harder to clean, ready to wear, easy to use*.

Some final points:

- All compound numbers should be hyphenated (e.g., *twenty-one, sixty-five, ninety-nine*).
- Hyphenate written fractions: *one-half, two-thirds, eight-tenths, seven-and-a-half miles*.
- A compound word beginning with *self* almost always requires a hyphen (e.g. *self-concept, self-esteem, self-made*). Exceptions are *selfish* and *selfless*.
- A hyphen is always required when a prefix is added to a capitalized term: *un-American, non-English, off-Broadway, Pre-Raphaelite, pan-Asian*.

One of the most useful sources of information for teachers on the correct use of hyphenation is the book titled *Collins: Improve your punctuation* (HarperCollins Publishers, 2009)—see particularly the chapters 'Hassles with hyphens' and 'A hotchpotch of hyphens'. Another valuable resource is *The Economist Style Guide* (10th ed., 2012), published by Profile Books, London.

An online search under 'use of hyphens' will also yield valuable information and examples. But you will also often find inconsistent advice—because there is still no single set of rules governing hyphenation upon which every expert can agree.

Glossary

affix: a word element (morpheme) such as a prefix or suffix attached to a base or root word.

allophone: one of a set of slightly different pronunciations of a given phoneme, conditioned by the adjoining sounds within the target word (the phonetic environment). For example, the articulation of the phoneme /t/ is slightly different in the words *star, touch, strong, that*.

antonym: a word opposite in meaning to another (e.g., *good* and *bad; rich* and *poor; tall* and *short*).

auditory perception: the process by which the brain interprets sound.

cognition: the mental processes that underpin perception, thinking and knowing.

consonant blend: a cluster of two or three consonants used together to produce a pronounceable unit within a word (e.g., br, tr, cl, pr, str, spr, scr). The separate common sounds of each of the two or three letters can be detected.

digraph: two letters used to represent one speech sound (e.g., ch, th, sh, wh). The separate common sound associated with each letter cannot be detected.

diphthong: a two-vowel sequence interpreted as a single vowel (e.g., the 'oi' in *boil;* the 'ae' in *Caesar;* 'au' in *haul;* 'oy' in *royal*). The two vowel sounds are articulated together in a continuous (gliding) motion while moving the mouth and lips. They are often referred to as 'gliding vowels'. There are said to be eight diphthongs in English spelling.

elision: the omission of sounds, syllables or words in spoken language.

etymology: the study of the origin and derivations of words.

grapheme: the written or printed equivalent representing a phoneme.

homographs: written words that share the same spelling but have different meaning (e.g., *lead* as in 'The *lead* weight was heavy to carry', or in 'Please *lead* the way up the path'; *wind* as in 'A strong *wind* blew last night' or 'Please *wind* the string around the rod').

homonyms: spoken words that sound the same and have the same spelling, but different meanings (see above).

homophone: a word that sounds the same as another word but has a different meaning and spelling (e.g., *meet* and *meat; aid* and *aide; aloud* and *allowed; write* and *right*).

morpheme: the smallest unit of meaning within a word (e.g., *play* is a single morpheme; *player* has two morphemes; *unplayable* has three morphemes).

morphology: the study of the structure of words.

onomatopoeia: the formation and pronunciation of a word that replicates the living sound associated with it (e.g., *pop, fizz, gush, cuckoo, clink, rumble*).

onset: the beginning sound in a single-syllable word (e.g., /h/ in *hang*; /s/ in *sat*). (See also under *rime*.)

orthography: the spelling system and principles in a language.

phoneme: a speech sound. There are said to be between 40 and 44 phonemes in spoken English. The variation in recorded number occurs mainly because of differences across regional accents and dialects. There are only 26 letters available to encode these phonemes, hence the need for digraphs, blends and diphthongs (and the fact that a single letter may signal more than one sound). The Initial Teaching Alphabet (ITA), popular in the 1960s but now rarely used, introduced a total of 44 symbols to equate with the 44 speech sounds.

phonemic awareness: functional knowledge that words are composed of separate sounds (phonemes), and the mental ability to identify and manipulate sounds in words.

phonics: a proven method of teaching reading and spelling that capitalizes on applying a knowledge of letter-to-sound correspondences. Synthetic phonics refers to building words from their constituent sounds. Analytic phonics refers to first learning letter-sound correspondences by taking apart known words in print.

phonogram: a letter, or common cluster of letters, representing a speech sound or syllable in print or writing.

phonology: the sound system that underpins a language.

prefix: a unit added to the front of a word usually to modify its meaning (e.g. *pro*active; *dis*appear).

rime: the middle vowel and all letters that follow it in a single-syllable word (e.g., /–op/ in *shop*; /–ost/ in *most*). Learning to identify onset and rime in simple words is a very important stage in early reading and spelling.

root word: a basic word stem which has meaning and is without affixes.

schwa: a vowel that is unvoiced and indeterminate within a spoken word (e.g., the 'e' in *system*, or the 'u' in *circus*).

semantics: the meaning of a sentence or text.

suffix: a unit added to the end of a word usually to modify its meaning (e.g., shopp*ing*)

synonym: a word having the same, or almost the same, meaning as another word (e.g., *small* and *little* and *tiny*; *thrilled* and *excited*; *noisy* and *rowdy*).

syntax: the rules that govern the construction of sentences in a language.

visual perception: the ability to interpret and process information taken in by the eyes.

References

Abbott, M. (2001). Effects of traditional versus extended word-study spelling instruction on students' orthographic knowledge. *Reading Online, 5*(3). Online article accessed 01 March 2013 at: http://www.readingonline.org/articles/art_index.asp?HREF=abbott/index.html

ACARA (Australian Curriculum and Assessment Authority). (2011a). *Foundation to Year 10 achievement standards in English, mathematics, science and history: Validation report.* Sydney, NSW: ACARA.

——(2011b). *Minimum standards: Spelling.* Online document accessed 19 October 2012 at: http://www.nap.edu.au/NAPLAN/About_each_domain/Language_Conventions/Minimum_standards_-_spelling/index.html

——(2012a). *The Australian Curriculum online.* Online document accessed 19 October 2012 at: http://www.australiancurriculum.edu.au/Search?q=spelling

——(2012b). *National Assessment Program—Literacy and Numeracy: Summary Report (Preliminary Results).* Sydney, NSW: ACARA.

——(2012c). *National Assessment Program: Achievement in reading, persuasive writing, language conventions and numeracy.* Sydney, NSW: ACARA.

Adams, M.J. (1990). *Beginning to read: Thinking and learning about print.* Cambridge, MA: MIT Press.

Adams-Gordon, B.L. (2010a). *The benefits of multisensory spelling instruction.* Pomeroy, WA: Castlemoyle Books.

——(2010b). *Spelling power* (4th ed.). Pomeroy, WA: Castlemoyle Books.

Alderman, G.L., and Green, S.K. (2011). Fostering lifelong spellers through meaningful experiences. *Reading Teacher, 64,* 8: 599–605.

Alphonso, C. (2013). Should I complain when my child's teachers make spelling and grammar mistakes? *Toronto Globe and Mail* (online), 17 January 2013.

Amtmann, D., Abbott, R.D., and Berninger, V.W. (2008). Identifying and predicting classes of response to explicit phonological spelling instruction during independent composing. *Journal of Learning Disabilities, 41,* 3: 218–234.

Anderson, W.F., and Stern, D. (1972). The relative effects of the Frostig Program, corrective reading instruction and attention, upon the reading skills of corrective readers with visual perceptual deficiencies. *Journal of School Psychology, 10,* 4: 387–395.

Apel, K. (2007). *Word study: Using a five-block approach to improving literacy skills.* Paper presented at *TSHA Conference,* 29 March 2007, Florida State University.

Arizona Department of Education. (2012). *Arizona's Common Core Standards: English Language Arts*. Online document accessed 11 October 2013 at: http://www.azed.gov/azcommoncore/elastandards/3-5ela/

Arndt, E.J. (2010). *Factors affecting the development of second grade spelling at the teacher, student, and word level*. Ph.D. Dissertation, Florida State University, College of Education. Online document accessed 11 October 2013 at: http://etd.lib.fsu.edu/theses/available/etd-01132010-092235/unrestricted/Arndt_E_Dissertation_2010.pdf

Arndt, E.J., and Foorman, B.R. (2009). *Students as spellers: What types of errors are they making?* Address to the International Dyslexia Association Annual Conference: www.fcrr.org/.../Arndt_IDA2009_StudentsasSpellers.ppt

Atkins, M., and Tierney, E. (2004). The relationship between memory skills (auditory and visual) and reading and spelling ability for a sample of children with specific learning disability. *Research Journal of Special Needs in Ireland, 17*, 2: 81–92.

Bahr, R.H., Silliman, E.R., Berninger, V.W., and Dow, M. (2012). Linguistic pattern analysis of misspellings of typically developing writers in Grades 1–9. *Journal of Speech, Language, and Hearing Research, 55*, 6: 1587–1599.

Ball, E.W., and Blachman, B.A. (1991). Does phoneme awareness in kindergarten make a difference in early word recognition and developmental spelling? *Reading Research Quarterly, 26*, 1: 49–66.

Bear, D.R., Invernizzi, M., and Johnson, F. (1995). *Words their way: Word study for phonics, vocabulary, and spelling instruction* (1st ed.). Englewood Cliffs, NJ: Pearson-Prentice-Hall.

Bear, D.R., Invernizzi, M., Templeton, S., and Johnson, F. (2012). *Words their way: Word study for phonics, vocabulary, and spelling instruction* (5th ed.). Englewood Cliffs, NJ: Pearson-Prentice-Hall.

Berninger, V.W., Lee, Y.L., Abbott, R.D., and Breznitz, Z. (2013). Teaching children with dyslexia to spell in a Reading-Writers' Workshop. *Annals of Dyslexia, 63*, 1: 1–24.

Bissaker, K., and Westwood, P. (2006). Diagnostic uses of the South Australian Spelling Test. *Australian Journal of Learning Disabilities, 11*, 1: 25–33.

Bradford, N. (2012). *MP sparks spelling debate*. Anglia ITV [UK]. Online document accessed 11 October 2013 at: http://www.itv.com/news/anglia/2012-05-11/mp-sparks-spelling-debate/

Bradley, L., and Bryant, P.E. (1983). *Rhyme and reason in reading and spelling*. Ann Arbor, MI: University of Michigan Press.

Breslauer, A.H., Mack, J.D., and Wilson, W.K. (1976). A visual-perceptual training program. *Intervention in School and Clinic, 11*, 3: 321–334.

Brooks, G. (2007). *What works for pupils with learning difficulties?* London: Department for Children, Schools and Families.

Bruck, M., Treiman, R., Caravolas, M., Genesee, F., and Cassar, M. (1998). Spelling skills of children in whole language and phonics classrooms. *Applied Psycholinguistics, 19*: 669–684.

Burt, J.S., and Fury, M.B. (2000). Spelling in adults: The role of reading skills and experience. *Reading and Writing, 13*, 1/2: 1–30.

Bus, A.G., and Van Ijzendoorn, M.H. (1999). Phonological awareness and early reading: A Meta-analysis of experimental training studies. *Journal of Educational Psychology, 91*, 403–414.

California Department of Education. (2009). *California Standards Tests*. Online document accessed 11 October 2013 at: http://www.cde.ca.gov/ta/tg/sr/documents/cstrtqela3nw.pdf

Callaghan, G., and Madelaine, A. (2012). Levelling the playing field for kindergarten entry: Research implications for preschool early literacy instruction. *Australasian Journal of Early Childhood, 37*, 1: 13–23.

Callard-Szulgit, R. (2012). *Perfectionism and gifted children* (2nd ed.). New York: Rowman and Littlefield.

Carlisle, J.F. (2010). Effects of instruction in morphological awareness on literacy achievement: An integrative review. *Reading Research Quarterly, 45*, 4: 464–487.

Carreker, S., and Birsh, J.R. (2011). *Multisensory teaching of basic language skills* (3rd ed.). Baltimore, MD: Brookes.

Carrillo, M.S., Alegria, J., and Marin, J. (2013). On the acquisition of some basic word spelling mechanisms in a deep (French) and a shallow (Spanish) system. *Reading and Writing: An Interdisciplinary Journal, 26*, 6: 799–819.

Carroll, J.M., Snowling, M.J., Hulme, C., and Stevenson, J. (2003). The development of phonological awareness in preschool children. *Developmental Psychology, 39*, 5: 913–923.

Cates, G.L., Dunne, M., Erkfritz, K.N., Kivisto, A., Lee, N., and Wierzbieki, J. (2007). Differential effects of two spelling procedures on acquisition and adaptation to reading. *Journal of Behavioral Education, 16*, 1: 71–81.

Chliounaki, K., and Bryant, P. (2007). How children learn about morphological spelling rules. *Child Development, 78*, 4: 1360–1373.

Cieslar, W., McLaughlin, T.F., and Derby, K.M. (2008). Effects of the copy, cover and compare procedure on the math and spelling performance of a high school student with behavioral disorder: A case report. *Preventing School Failure, 52*, 4: 45–51.

Conrad, N.J. (2008). From reading to spelling and spelling to reading: Transfer goes both ways. *Journal of Educational Psychology, 100*, 4: 869–878.

Cook, J.L. (2003). *The effects of word sorting on spelling retention*. MA(Ed) Dissertation, Viterbo University, La Crosse, WI.

Cook, L. (2011). *Effects of multisensory instruction on spelling in second grade*. Online research report accessed on 04 March 2013 at: www.ltl.appstate.edu/prodlearn/prodlearn/POL_summer_2011/...

Cooke, A. (1997). Learning to spell difficult words: Why look, cover, write and check is not enough. *Dyslexia, 3*: 240–243.

Cooke, N.L., Slee, J.M., and Young, C.A. (2008). How is contextualized spelling used to support reading in first-grade core reading programs? *Reading Improvement, 45*, 1: 26–45.

Cripps, C. (1990). Teaching joined writing to children on school entry as an agent for catching spelling. *Australian Journal of Remedial Education, 22*, 3: 13–15.

Crouse, J., and Landers, G. (2011). *Word Sorts: Building alphabetic and phonic knowledge*. Online research report accessed 01 March 2013 at: http://www.appstate.edu/~koppenhaverd/rcoe/f11/5040/papers/jennifer&ginger.pdf

Crowley, K., Mayer, P., and Stuart-Hamilton, I. (2009). Changes in reliance on reading and spelling sub-skills across the lifespan. *Educational Gerontology, 35*, 6: 503–522.

Crystal, D. (2005). *The stories of English*. New York: Overlook Press.

——(2011). *The story of English in 100 words.* London: Profile Books.

——(2012). *Spell it out: The singular story of English spelling.* London: Profile Books.

Cunningham, P. (1995). *Phonics they use.* Columbus, OH: Pearson-Allyn & Bacon.

——(2011). *What matters in spelling: Research-based strategies.* Columbus, OH: Pearson.

Cutts, M. (2009). *Oxford guide to plain English* (3rd ed.). Oxford, UK: Oxford University Press.

Dahl, K., and Associates. (2003). Connecting developmental word study with classroom writing: Children's descriptions of spelling strategies. *The Reading Teacher, 57,* 4: 310–319.

Darch, C., Kim, S., Johnson, S., and James, H. (2000). The strategic spelling skills of students with learning disabilities: The results of two studies. *Journal of Instructional Psychology, 27,* 1: 15–26.

Davies, A. (2006). *Teaching THRASS.* Chester, UK: THRASS UK.

Davis, B.G. (2013). *Research-based spelling: Sitton spelling and word study.* Online article accessed 25 February 2013 at: http://eps.schoolspecialty.com/downloads/research_papers/series/SSWS_research.pdf

Davis, C. (1999). Spelling and literacy in Finnish. *Journal of the Simplified Spelling Society, 25,* 1: 11–15.

Davis, K.N. (2011). *A comparative content analysis of five spelling programs in the 1st, 3rd, and 5th grade.* Ed.D Dissertation, San Diego State University. Online document accessed 11 October 2013, 06 January 2013 at: http://sdsu-dspace.calstate.edu/bitstream/handle/10211.10/1062/Davis_Katherine.pdf?sequence=1

Davison, S. (2001). *Go Phonics.* Chelan, WA: Foundations for Learning.

de Graaff, S., Bosman, A.T., Hasselman, F., and Verhoeven, L. (2009). Benefits of systematic phonics instruction. *Scientific Studies of Reading, 13,* 4: 318–333.

Dehaene, S. (2009). *Reading in the brain: The science and evolution of a human invention.* New York: Viking/Penguin.

DET [NSW]. [Department of Education and Training, New South Wales]. (2009). *Literacy teaching guide: Phonics.* Sydney: DET.

Devonshire, V., Morris, P., and Fluck, M. (2013). Spelling and reading development: The effect of teaching children multiple levels of representation in their orthography. *Learning and Instruction, 25:* 85–94.

Dew, T. (2012). *Word Study: A look at improving learning and retention of spelling.* ERIC Online document accessed 04 January 2013 at: http://www.eric.ed.gov/ERICWebPortal/search/recordDetails.jsp?ERICExtSearch_SearchValue_0=ED114839&ERICExtSearch_SearchType_0=no&_pageLabel=RecordDetails&accno=ED535985&_nfls=false

DfE [Department for Education: UK]. (2012a). *New primary curriculum to bring higher standards in English, maths and science.* Online press notice 210127, June 2012.

——(2012b). *National Curriculum for English Key Stages 1 and 2: Draft.* London: The Department.

Diaz, I. (2010). *The effect of morphological instruction in improving the spelling, vocabulary, and reading comprehension of high school English language learners (ELLs).* ProQuest LLC, Ph.D. Dissertation, TUI University. (ERIC Document ED514872.)

Dich, N., and Pedersen, B. (2013). Native language effects in spelling in English as a foreign language: A time-course analysis. *Canadian Journal of Applied Linguistics, 16*, 1: 51–68.

Draper, D. (2008). *Thinking spelling.* Online resource accessed 21 January 2012 at: http://www.decd.sa.gov.au/barossa/files/links/thinkingspelling.pdf

Duff, F.J., Hayiou-Thomas, M.E., and Hulme, C. (2012). Evaluating the effectiveness of a phonologically based reading intervention for struggling readers with varying language profiles. *Reading and Writing: An Interdisciplinary Journal, 25*, 3: 621–640.

Ecalle, J., Magnan, A., Bouchafa, H., and Gombert, J.E. (2009). Computer-based training with ortho-phonological units in dyslexic children: New investigations. *Dyslexia, 15*, 3: 218–238.

Eden, S., Shamir, A., and Fershtman, M. (2011). The effect of using laptops on the spelling skills of students with learning disabilities. *Educational Media International, 48*, 4: 249–259.

Ehri, L.C. (1997). Learning to read and learning to spell are one and the same, almost. In C.A. Perfetti, L. Rieben, and M. Fayol (Eds.), *Learning to spell: Research, theory, and practice across languages* (pp.237–269). Mahwah, NJ: Erlbaum.

——(2000). Learning to read and learning to spell: Two sides of a coin. *Topics in Language Disorders, 20*, 3: 19–36.

Ehri, L.C., and Wilce, L. (1985). Movement into reading: Is the first stage of printed word learning visual or phonetic? *Reading Research Quarterly, 20*: 163–179.

Erion, J., Davenport, C., Rodax, N., Scholl, B., and Hardy, J. (2009). Cover-Copy-Compare and spelling: One versus three repetitions. *Journal of Behavioral Education, 18*, 4: 319–330.

Farkas, R.D. (2003). The effects of traditional versus learning-styles instructional methods in middle years. *The Journal of Educational Research, 97*, 1: 42–54.

Fennema-Jansen, S. (2001). Measuring effectiveness: Technology to support writing. *Special Education Technology Practice, 3*, 1: 16–22.

Fielding-Barnsley, R. (2010). Australian pre-service teachers' knowledge of phonemic awareness and phonics in the process of learning to read. *Australian Journal of Learning Difficulties, 15*, 1: 99–110.

Fisher, B., Bruce, M., and Greive, C. (2007). Look-Say-Cover-Write-Say-Check and Old Way/New Way meditational learning: A comparison of the effectiveness of two tutoring programs for children with persistent spelling difficulties. *Special Eduction Perspectives, 16*, 1: 19–38.

Fletcher-Flinn, C., Elmes, H., and Strugnell, D. (1997). Visual-perceptual and phonological factors in acquisition of literacy among children with congenital developmental coordination disorders. *Developmental Medicine and Child Neurology, 39*, 3: 158–166.

Foorman, B.R., and Petscher, Y. (2010). Development of spelling and differential relations to text reading in Grades 3–12. *Assessment for Effective Intervention, 36*, 1: 7–20.

Fountas, I.C., and Pinnell, G.S. (2004). *Word study lessons: Phonics, spelling, and vocabulary.* Portsmouth, NH: Heinemann.

Fresch, M.J. (2003). A national survey of spelling instruction: Investigating teachers' beliefs and practices. *Journal of Literacy Research, 35*, 3: 819–848.

Fresch, M.J., and Wheaton, A. (2002). *Teaching and assessing spelling.* New York: Scholastic Professional Books.

Frith, U. (1982). *Cognitive processes in spelling and their relevance to spelling reform.* Paper presented at the Third International Conference on Reading and Spelling. Online document accessed 29 December 2012 at: http://www.spellingsociety.org/bulletins/b82/spring/hrh.php

Frostig, M., and Horne, D. (1964). *The Frostig program for the development of visual perception.* Chicago: Follett.

Gagen, M. (2010). *Effective spelling instruction.* Online document accessed 11 October 2013 at: http://www.righttrackreading.com/howtospell.html

Galletly, S.A., and Knight, B.A. (2013). Because trucks aren't bicycles: Orthographic complexity as an important variable in reading research. *Australian Educational Researcher, 40,* 2: 173–194.

Ganske, K. (2000). *Word journeys.* New York: Guilford Press.

——(2006). *Word sorts and more.* New York: Guilford Press.

——(2008). *Mindful of words: Spelling and vocabulary explorations.* New York: Guilford Press.

Gentry, J.R. (1978). Early spelling strategies. *The Elementary School Journal, 79,* 2: 88–92.

Gentry, J.R. (1987). *Spel... is a four-letter word.* Portsmouth, NH: Heinemann.

——(2000). *Five questions teachers ask about spelling.* Zane-Bloser. Interview with J.R. Gentry. Online document accessed 11 October 2013 at: http://www.zaner-bloser.com/news/five-questions-teachers-ask-about-spelling

——(2010). Readers, writers and spellers. *Psychology Today* (online). Online document accessed 11 October 2013 at: http://www.psychologytoday.com/blog/raising-readers-writers-and-spellers/201008/no-spelling-book-in-your-child-s-book-bag-spells-tr

——(2011). Bring weekly spelling tests back. *Psychology Today* (online). Online document accessed 11 October 2013 at: http://www.psychologytoday.com/blog/raising-readers-writers-and-spellers/201103/bring-weekly-spelling-tests-back

Gillingham, A., and Stillman, B. (1960). *Remedial teaching for children with specific disability in reading, spelling and penmanship.* Cambridge, MA: Educators Publishing Service.

Gioia, C. (2008). *How to improve your spelling.* Online document accessed 04 March 2013 at: http://www.helium.com/items/1180317-how-to-improve-your-spelling

GL Assessments. (2008). *British Spelling Test Series.* London: GL Education Group.

Goldfus, C. (2012). Knowledge foundations for beginning reading teachers in EFL. *Annals of Dyslexia, 62,* 3: 204–221.

Goldstein, S., and Schwebach, A. (2009). Neuropsychological basis of learning disabilities. In C.R. Reynolds and E. Fletcher-Janzen (Eds.) *Handbook of clinical child neurology* (3rd ed., pp.187–202). New York: Springer.

Gov.UK. (2013). *The National Curriculum Guide.* Online document accessed 30 March 2013 at: https://www.gov.uk/national-curriculum/overview

Graham, S. (1999). Handwriting and spelling instruction for students with learning disabilities: A review. *Learning Disability Quarterly, 22,* 2: 78–98.

Graham, S., Harris, K., and Loynachan, C. (1996). The Directed Spelling Thinking Activity: Application with high-frequency words. *Learning Disabilities: Research and Practice, 11,* 1: 34–40.

Groff, P. (1995). Handwriting and its relationship to spelling. *Journal of the Simplified Spelling Society, 19*, 2: 22–25.

——(2007). *A critique of inventive spelling.* Paper available on the National Right to Read Foundation. Online document accessed 28 February 2013 at: http://www.nrrf.org/42_invented_spelling.html

Gursky, K. (2003). *Interactive Words Walls.* A contribution displayed on The School Bell website. Online document accessed 08 March 2013 at: http://www.theschoolbell.com/Links/word_walls/words.html

Harrison, G.L. (2005). The spelling strategies of students with varying graphophonemic skills: Implications for instruction and intervention. *Exceptionality Education Canada, 15*, 3: 57–76.

Henderson, E.H., and Beers, J. (Eds.). (1980). *Developmental and cognitive aspects of learning to spell.* Newark, DE: International Reading Association.

Hendrickson, H. (1967). *Spelling: A visual skill. A discussion of visual imagery and the manipulation of visual symbols as basic skills in the ability to spell.* Rafael, CA: Academic Therapy Publications.

Henry, M.K. (2010). *Unlocking literacy: Effective decoding and spelling instruction* (2nd ed.). Baltimore, MD: Brookes.

Hepplewhite, D. (2008). *Teaching spelling: How to.* Online article on the Teaching Expertise website, accessed 27 November 2012 at: http://www.teachingexpertise.com/articles/teaching-spelling-how-5079

Hetzroni, O.E., and Shrieber, B. (2004). Word processing as an assistive technology tool for enhancing academic outcomes for students with writing difficulties in the general classroom. *Journal of Learning Disabilities, 37*, 2: 143–154.

Hilte, M., and Reitsma, P. (2006). Spelling pronunciation and visual preview both facilitate learning to spell irregular words. *Annals of Dyslexia, 56*: 301–318.

Holland, K. (2012). Vision and learning. In L. Peer and G. Reid (Eds.) *Special educational needs: A guide to inclusive practice* (pp.112–126). London: SAGE Publications.

Holmes, V.M., and Babauta, M.L. (2005). Single or dual representations for reading and spelling? *Reading and Writing: An Interdisciplinary Journal, 18*, 3: 257–280.

Hook, P.E., and Jones, S.D. (2002). The importance of automaticity and fluency for efficient reading comprehension. *Perspectives: International Dyslexia Association Newsletter, 28*, 1: 9–14.

Hudson, J.S., and Toler, L. (1949). Instruction in auditory and visual discrimination as means of improving spelling. *The Elementary School Journal, 49*, 8: 466–469.

Hutcheon, G., Campbell, M., and Stewart, J. (2012). Spelling instruction through etymology: A method of developing spelling lists for older students. *Australian Journal of Educational and Developmental Psychology, 12*: 60–70.

Jackson, C.C. (2008). *Let's All Spell: An independently conducted inquiry into the teaching of spelling and remedial spelling in New Zealand schools.* Wellington, NZ: Privately Published Report.

——(2012). *'Fonetik': Teaching the basic skills to spell a word phonetically.* Online article accessed 11 November 2012 at: http://ezispel.co.nz/index.htm

Jaspers, K.E., Williams, R.L., Skinner, C., Cihak, D., McCallum, R.S., and Ciancio, D.J. (2012). How and to what extent do two Cover, Copy, and Compare spelling interventions contribute to spelling, word recognition, and vocabulary development? *Journal of Behavioral Education, 21*, 1: 80–98.

Johnson, A.P. (1998). Word Class: Using thinking skills to enhance spelling instruction. *Reading Horizons, 38,* 4: 257–265.

Johnson, D., and Obi, S.C. (1993). *Mnemonics: Can you spell it?* ERIC online document ED394220.

Johnston, F. (1999). The timing and teaching of word families. *Reading Teacher, 53,* 1: 64–76.

Johnston, R.S., McGeown, S., and Watson, J.E. (2012). Long-term effects of synthetic versus analytic phonics teaching on the reading and spelling ability of 10-year-old boys and girls. *Reading and Writing: An Interdisciplinary Journal, 25,* 6: 1365–1384.

Johnston, R.S., and Watson, J. (2003). Accelerating reading and spelling with synthetic phonics: A five year follow-up. *Insight 4.* Edinburgh: Scottish Executive Education Department.

Jones, S. (2009). *Importance of spelling.* Fort Lauderdale, FL: Vocabulary SpellingCity. com website. Online article accessed 23 November 2012 at: http://www.spellingcity. com/importance-of-spelling.html

Joseph, L., and Orlins, A. (2005). Multiple uses of word study technique. *Reading Improvement, 42,* 2: 73–79.

Joshi, R.M., and Aaron, P.G. (2005). Spelling: Assessment and instructional recommendations. *Perspectives on Language and Literacy* [International Dyslexia Association], 31, 3: 38–41.

Joshi, R.M., Treiman, R., Carreker, S., and Moats, L.C. (2009). How words cast their spell: Spelling is an integral part of learning the language, not a matter of memorization. *American Educator, 32,* 4: 6–43.

Kagohara, D.M., Sigafoos, J., Achmadi, D., O'Reilly, M., and Lancioni, G. (2012). Teaching children with autism spectrum disorders to check the spelling of words. *Research in Autism Spectrum Disorders, 6,* 1: 304–310.

Kast, M., Baschera, G., Gross, M., Jancke, L., and Meyer, M. (2011). Computer-based learning of spelling skills in children with and without dyslexia. *Annals of Dyslexia, 61,* 2: 177–200.

Keesbury, F.E. (2007). Frostig Remedial Program. In C.R. Reynolds and E. Fletcher-Janzen (Eds.). *Encyclopedia of special education* (pp.926–927). Hoboken, NJ: Wiley.

Keller, C. (2002). A new twist on spelling instruction for elementary school teachers. *Intervention in School and Clinic 38,* 1: 3–8.

Kemper, M.J., Verhoeven, L., and Bosman, A.M.T. (2012). Implicit and explicit teaching of spelling rules. *Learning and Individual Differences, 22,* 6: 639–649.

Khamsi, R. (2007). Tricky spelling drains the brain, *New Scientist* (online) 27 April 2007. Online article accessed 21 January 2013 at: http://www.newscientist.com/article/dn11731-tricky-spelling-drains-the-brain.html

Kingsley, K.A. (2012). 'From spelling to word study': A word study approach for the elementary classroom. *ETD collection for University of Nebraska–Lincoln.* Online document accessed 11 October 2013 at http://digitalcommons.unl.edu/dissertations/AAI3494721

Kohnen, S., Nickels, L., and Castles, A. (2009). Assessing spelling skills and strategies: A critique of available resources. *Australian Journal of Learning Difficulties, 14,* 1: 113–150.

Kraai, R.V. (2011). *Metacognitive strategy use in second grade students with learning disabilities during written spelling tasks* (Monograph). ProQuest UMI Dissertation Publishing.

Krashen, S. (2002). *The reading-spelling connection.* Online document accessed 21 February 2013 at: http://www.trelease-on-reading.com/spelling-krashen.html

Leipzig, D.H. (2000). The knowledge base for Word Study: What teachers need to know. *Scientific Studies of Reading, 11,* 2: 105–131.

Levy, L.S. (2011). *Hear It, Say It, Spell It: Investigating non-visual pathways for spelling.* Online report accessed 31 January 2013 at: http://www.amstat.org/education/posterprojects/projects/2008/3-Grades7-9-SecondPlace.pdf

Lewis, N. (1978). *Word power made easy.* New York: Simon & Schuster Pocket Books.

Lipson, M., and Wixson, K. (2012). *Assessment and instruction of reading and writing* (5th ed.). Boston, MA: Pearson.

Lloyd, S., and Lib, S. (2000). *The phonics handbook: Jolly phonics.* Chigwell, UK: Jolly Learning Ltd.

Loeffler, K.A. (2005). No more Friday spelling tests? An alternative spelling assessment for students with learning disabilities. *Teaching Exceptional Children, 37,* 4: 24–27.

Logsdon, A. (2013). *Make multisensory teaching materials.* Online article on the About.Com Learning Disabilities website, accessed 04 March 2013 at: http://learningdisabilities.about.com/od/instructionalmaterials/p/mulitsensory.htm

Lonigan, C.J., and Shanahan, T. (2008). *Developing early literacy: Report of the National Early Literacy Panel (Executive Summary).* Washington, DC: National Institute for Literacy.

Lutz, E. (1986). Invented spelling and spelling development. *Language Arts, 63,* 7: 742–744.

Lyndon, H. (1989). 'I did it my way': An introduction to Old Way/New Way. *Australasian Journal of Special Education, 13:* 32–37.

MacArthur, C.A., Graham, S., Haynes, J.B., and DeLaPaz, S. (1996). Spelling checkers and students with learning disabilities: Performance comparisons and impact on spelling. *The Journal of Special Education, 30,* 1: 35–57.

McCabe, D. (1997). *Speech to spelling.* Birch Run, MI: AVKO Educational Research Foundation.

McCloskey, M. (2009). *Visual reflections: A perceptual deficit and its implications.* Oxford, UK: Oxford University Press.

Mann, T.B. Bushell, D., and Morris, E.K. (2010). Use of sounding out to improve spelling in young children. *Journal of Applied Behavior Analysis, 43,* 1: 89–93.

Manning, B., and Tibshraeny, J. (2013). Spelling trouble in our classes. *Bay of Plenty Times* (online). Online article accessed 28 February 2013 at: http://www.bayofplentytimes.co.nz/news/spelling-trouble-in-our-classes/1772019/

Manning, M., and Underbakke, C. (2005). Spelling development research necessitates replacement of weekly word lists. *Childhood Education, 81,* 4: 236–238.

Marszalek, J. (2012). Teachers get an 'F' for spelling. *The Australian* (online). Online article accessed 22 October 2012. http://www.theaustralian.com.au/news/teachers-get-f-for-spelling/story-e6frg6n6-1226500296664

Maslanka, P., and Joseph, L.M. (2002). A comparison of two phonological awareness techniques between samples of preschool children. *Reading Psychology, 23,* 4: 271–288.

Massengill, D. (2006). Mission accomplished—it's learnable now: Voices of mature challenged spellers using a Word Study approach. *Journal of Adolescent and Adult Literacy, 49,* 5: 420–431.

Massey, A., and Dexter, T. (2002). *An evaluation of spelling, punctuation and grammar assessments in GCSE.* Paper presented at the British Educational Research Association Annual Conference, Exeter University, September 2002.

Matchan, L. (2012). Defying societal habits, spelling regains its dignity. *The Boston Globe* (online) 09 January 2012. Online article accessed 24 November 2012 at: http://www.boston.com/lifestyle/articles/2012/01/09/spelling_becomes_popular_again/?page=1

MDE [Minnesota Department of Education]. (2010). *Minnesota Academic Standards: English Language Arts K-12.* Online document accessed 30 March 2013 at: http://education.state.mn.us/MDE/EdExc/StanCurri/K-12AcademicStandards/index.htm

Meehan, R., and Hammond, L. (2006). Walking the talk: Western Australian teachers' beliefs about early reading and spelling instruction and their knowledge of metalinguistics. *Australian Journal of Learning Disabilities, 11,* 1: 17–24.

Melby-Lervåg, M., Lyster, S-A.H., and Hulme, C. (2012). Phonological skills and their role in learning to read: A meta-analytic review. *Psychological Bulletin, 138:* 322–352.

Ministry of Education [New Zealand]. (2013). *National Education Monitoring Project.* Online document accessed 14 March 2013 at: http://www.educationcounts.govt.nz/topics/research/nemp

Moats, L.C. (2005). How spelling supports reading. *American Educator*, Winter Issue 2005/06: 12–43.

——(2009). Teaching spelling to students with language and learning disabilities. In G.A. Troia (Ed.) *Instruction and assessment for struggling writers: Evidence-based practices* (pp.269–289). New York: Guilford Press.

——(2010). *How should spelling be assessed?* Online article accessed 15 March 2013 at: http://louisamoats.wordpress.com/category/spelling/

Montgomery, D. (2005). *Cohort analysis of writing in Year 7 following 2, 4 and 7 years of the National Literacy Strategy.* Paper presented at the British Educational Research Association Annual Conference, University of Glamorgan, 14–17 September 2005.

——(2012). The contribution of handwriting and spelling remediation to overcoming dyslexia. In T. Wydell (Ed.) *Dyslexia: A comprehensive and international approach* (pp.109–146). Manhattan, NY: InTech. Online article accessed 04 January 2013 at: http://cdn.intechopen.com/pdfs/35808/InTech-The_contribution_of_handwriting_and_spelling_remediation_to_overcoming_dyslexia.pdf

Morris, H., and Smith, S. (2011). *33 ways to help with spelling.* London: Routledge.

Morris, S. (2013). School standards in Wales causing concern. *The Guardian Online.* Online article accessed 29 January 2013 at: http://www.guardian.co.uk/education/2013/jan/29/school-standards-wales-causing-concern

Moseley, D. (1997). Assessment of spelling and related aspects of written expression. In J.R Beech and C. Singleton (Eds.) *The psychological assessment of reading.* London: Routledge.

Moser, L.A., Fishley, K.M., Konrad, M., and Hessler, T. (2012). Effects of the Copy-Cover-Compare strategy on acquisition, maintenance, and generalization of spelling sight words for elementary students with Attention Deficit/Hyperactivity Disorder. *Child & Family Behavior Therapy, 34*, 2: 93–110.

Mullock, B. (2012). An examination of commercial spelling programs for upper primary level students. *Australasian Journal of Special Education, 36*, 2: 172–195.

Murray, B., and Steinen, M. (2011). Word-map-ping: How understanding spellings improves spelling power. *Intervention in School and Clinic, 46*, 5: 299–304.

NCFOT [National Centre for Fair and Open Testing: US]. (2008). *Test scores unreliable means of assessing school quality.* Online document accessed 31 March 2013 at: http://www.fairtest.org/test-scores-unreliable-means-assessing-school-qual

NCLD [National Center for Learning Disabilities]. (2008). *Visual processing disorders.* Online document accessed 24 December 2012 at: http://www.ldonline.org/article/25152/

NCTE [National Council of Teachers of English]. (2012). *NCTE/IRA Standards for the English Language Arts.* Online document accessed 11 October 2013 at: http://www.ncte.org/standards/ncte-ira

Newingham, B. (2010). *My November top ten list: Word Study in action.* Online article accessed 11 October 2013 at: http://www.scholastic.com/teachers/top_teaching/2010/10/my-november-top-ten-list-word-study-in-action

Nichols, R. (1985). *Helping your child spell.* Reading, UK: University of Reading.

Nies, K.A., and Belfiore, P.J. (2006). Enhancing spelling performance in students with learning disabilities. *Journal of Behavioral Education, 15*, 3: 162–169.

Nordquist, R. (2011). *Twenty spelling mnemonics.* Online document, available on About.com website, accessed 05 March 2013 at: http://grammar.about.com/b/2011/05/27/twenty-spelling-mnemonics.htm

——(2012). *Top four spelling rules.* Online document, available on About.com website, accessed 17 February 2013 at: http://grammar.about.com/od/words/tp/spellrules.htm

Norton, E.S., Kovelman, I., and Petitto, L.A. (2007). Are there separate neural systems for spelling? New insights into the role of rules and memory in spelling from fMRI. *International Journal of Mind, Brain & Education, 1*, 1: 48–56.

Nunes, T., Bryant, P., and Bindman, M. (1997). Morphological spelling strategies: Developmental stages and processes. *Developmental Psychology, 33*, 4: 637–649.

OSPI [Office of Superintendent of Public Instruction] Washington. (2010). *Common Core Standards for Language Arts.* Online document accessed 11 October 2013 at: http://www.k12.wa.us/CoreStandards/ELAstandards/pubdocs/CCSSI_ELA_Standards.pdf#9

Ott, P. (2007). *Teaching children with dyslexia.* London: Routledge.

Papen, U., Watson, K., and Marriot, N. (2012). *The phonological influences on children's spelling.* Online document from the Department of Linguistics and English Language, University of Lancaster, accessed 08 February 2013 at: http://www.lancs.ac.uk/fss/linguistics/staff/kevin/spelling.htm

Peters, M.L. (1970). *Success in spelling.* Cambridge, UK: Cambridge Institute of Education.

——(1974). The significance of spelling miscues. In B. Wade and K. Wedell (Eds.) *Spelling: Task and learner.* Birmingham, UK: University of Birmingham Press.

——(1985). *Spelling: Caught or taught? A new look.* London: Routledge.

Phillips, W.E., and Feng, J. (2012). *Methods for sight word recognition in kindergarten: Traditional flashcard method vs. multisensory approach.* Research Report presented at Georgia Educational Research Association Conference, Savannah, GA, 18–20 October 2012.

Prior, M., Frye, S., and Fletcher, C. (1987). Remediation for subgroups of retarded readers using a modified oral spelling procedure. *Developmental Medicine and Child Neurology, 29*, 1: 64–71.

Puranik, C.S., and Alotaiba, S. (2012). Examining the contribution of handwriting and spelling to written expression in kindergarten children. *Reading and Writing: An Interdisciplinary Journal, 25*, 7: 1523–1546.

Puranik, C.S., Lonigan, C.J., and Kim, Y.S. (2011). Contributions of emergent literacy skills to name writing, letter writing, and spelling in preschool children. *Early Childhood Research Quarterly, 26*, 4: 465–474.

Ralston, M., and Robinson, G. (1997). Spelling strategies and metacognitive awareness in skilled and unskilled spellers. *Australian Journal of Learning Disabilities, 2*, 4: 12–23.

Rapp, B., and Lipka, K. (2011). The literate brain: The relationship between spelling and reading. *Journal of Cognitive Neuroscience 23*, 5: 1180–1197.

Rasinski, T., and Zutell, J. (2010). *Essential strategies for word study.* New York: Scholastic Teaching Resources.

Reed, D.K. (2012). *Why teach spelling?* Portsmouth, NH: Center on Instruction/RMC Research Corporation. Online document accessed 11 October 2012 at: http://www.centeroninstruction.org/files/Why%20Teach%20Spelling.pdf

Reis-Frankfort, T. (2013). *New buzz word for 'tricky words' in the new National Curriculum.* Online article accessed 02 March 2013 at: http://phonicbooks.wordpress.com/2013/01/20/new-buzz-word-for-tricky-words-in-the-new-national-curriculum/

Riggs, E.R. (2008). *Multi-sensory approaches to spelling and reading instruction for students with learning disabilities.* MEd Dissertation, College of Education, Ohio University.

Rippel, M. (2013). *Why we teach reading and spelling separately.* Eagle River: WI: All About Learning Press. Online article accessed 30 March 2013 at: http://www.allaboutlearningpress.com/why-we-teach-reading-and-spelling-separately

Rittle-Johnson, B., and Siegler, R.S. (1999). Learning to spell: Variability, choice and change in children's strategy use. *Child Development, 70*, 2: 332–348.

Robbins, L., and Kenny, H. (2007). *A sound approach: Using phonemic awareness to teach reading and spelling.* Winnipeg, Canada: Portage and Main Press.

Roberts, D. (2012). *Spelling With Imagery (SWIM).* Online document accessed 27 December 2012 at: http://www.psych-online.co.uk/p3s.html

Roberts, J. (2001). *Spelling recovery: The pathway to spelling success.* Melbourne: Australian Council for Educational Research.

Robinson, S. (2010). *The effects of embedded phonological awareness training on the reading and spelling skills of kindergarten students.* ProQuest LLC, Ph.D. Dissertation, University of North Dakota. ERIC online document ED522753.

Rook, R. (2012). *Effects of an interactive approach to word study versus a traditional spelling approach.* Ann Arbor, MI: ProQuest, UMI Dissertation Publishing. UMI 1466304.

Rose, J. (2009). *Identifying and teaching children and young people with dyslexia and literacy difficulties.* Nottingham, UK: DCSF Publications.

Rosenthal, J., and Ehri, L.C. (2011). Pronouncing new words aloud during the silent reading of text enhances fifth graders' memory for vocabulary words and their spellings. *Reading and Writing: An Interdisciplinary Journal, 24*, 8: 921–950.

Rutner, D. (2012). *Visual perceptual skills.* Online document on the Ezra Medical Center website (Brooklyn, NY), accessed 15 December 2012 at: http://www. ezramedical.org/article.html?a=16129

Sacre, L., and Masterson, J. (2000). *Single Word Spelling Test.* London: NfER-Nelson.

Sanchez, M., Magnan, A., and Ecalle, J. (2012). Knowledge about word structure in beginning readers: What specific links are there with word reading and spelling? *European Journal of Psychology of Education, 27*, 3: 299–317.

Santoro, L.E., Coyne, M.D., and Simmons, D.C. (2006). The reading–spelling connection: Developing and evaluating a beginning spelling intervention for children at risk of reading disability. *Learning Disabilities Research & Practice, 21*, 2: 122–133.

Saxon Publishing. (2004). *Saxon Phonics and Spelling.* Norman, OK: Saxon.

Schäffler, T., Sonntag, J., Hartnegg, K., and Fischer, B. (2004). The effect of practice on low-level auditory discrimination, phonological skills, and spelling in dyslexia. *Dyslexia, 10*, 2: 119–130.

Schlagal, B. (2002). Classroom spelling instruction: History, research and practice. *Reading Research and Instruction, 42*, 1: 44–57.

Schroeder, H.H. (1968). *An analysis of the use of visual and auditory perception in spelling instruction.* Ph.D. Dissertation, University of Iowa. University Microfilms (Xerox), Ann Arbor, MI.

Scott, C.M., and Brown, S.L. (2001). Spelling and the speech-language pathologist: There's more than meets the eye. *Seminars in Speech and Language, 22*, 3: 197–206.

Scott, R.M. (2010). *Word study instruction: Research into Practice Monograph 27.* Ontario, Canada: The Literacy and Numeracy Secretariat.

Scott-Dunne, D. (2012). *When spelling matters.* Markham, Ontario, Canada: Pembroke.

Scraper, K. (2002). *Word study through sorting.* Online article on the Educators Publishing Service website, accessed 1 March 2013 at: http://eps.schoolspecialty. com/downloads/articles/word_study_through_sorting.pdf

Sharp, A.C., Sinatra, G.M., and Reynolds, R.E. (2008). The development of children's orthographic knowledge: A microgenetic perspective. *Reading Research Quarterly, 43*, 3: 206–226.

Shmidman, A., and Ehri, L.C. (2010). Embedded picture mnemonics to learn letters. *Scientific Studies of Reading, 14*, 2: 159–182.

Sipe, R.B. (2008). Teaching challenged spellers in high school English classrooms. *English Journal, 97*, 4: 38–44.

Standards and Testing Agency [UK]. (2012). *English grammar, punctuation and spelling test framework: 2013–2015.* London: Department for Education.

Steffler, D.J. (2001). Implicit cognition and spelling development. *Developmental Review, 21*: 168–204.

Stirling, J. (2011a). *Teaching spelling to English language learners.* Raleigh, NC: Lulu Press.

——(2011b). *Spelling tests: A necessary evil?* Online article accessed 10 March 2013 at: http://thespellingblog.blogspot.com/2011/01/spelling-tests-necessary-evil.html

Stuart, M. (1999). Getting ready for reading: Early phoneme awareness and phonics teaching improves reading and spelling in inner-city second language learners. *British Journal of Educational Psychology, 69*: 587–605.

Sumner, E., Connelly, V., and Barnett, A.L. (2013). Children with dyslexia are slow writers because they pause more often and not because they are slow at handwriting execution. *Reading and Writing: An Interdisciplinary Journal, 26, 5*: 991–1008.

Tangel, D.M., and Blachman, B.A. (1995). Effect on phonemic awareness instruction on the invented spelling of first-grade children: A one-year follow-up. *Journal of Reading Behavior, 27*: 153–185.

Taylor, L.S. (2004). *Spelling: A lost art.* Online document accessed 25 March 2013 at: http://www.lewrockwell.com/taylor/taylor79.html

Templeton, S. (2000). *Teaching of spelling – the nature of the spelling system: A brief history of spelling instruction in the United States.* Online document accessed 03 December 2012 at: http://education.stateuniversity.com/pages/2441/Spelling-Teaching.html#ixzz2E84xb0Im

Templeton, S., and Morris, D. (2001). Reconceptualizing spelling development and instruction. *Reading Online, 5, 3.* Online article accessed on 01 January 2013 at: http://www.readingonline.org/articles/art_index.asp?HREF=/articles/handbook/templeton/index.html

TESS [The English Spelling Society]. (2005). *Why English spelling should be updated.* Online article accessed 05 October 2013 at: http://www.spellingsociety.org/aboutsss/leaflets/whyeng.php

Tompkins, G.E. (2010a). *Teaching spelling.* Online article accessed 24 February 2013 at: http://www.education.com/reference/article/teaching-spelling/

——(2010b). *Stages of spelling development.* Online article available on the Education. com website, accessed 10 March 2013 at: http://www.education.com/reference/article/stages-spelling-development/?page=3

Topfer, C., and Arendt, D. (2009). *Guiding thinking for effective spelling.* Melbourne: Education Services Australia.

Torgerson, C., Brooks, G., and Hall, J. (2006). *A systematic review of the research literature on the use of phonics in the teaching of reading and spelling. Research Report 711.* London: Department for Education and Skills.

Toutanova, K., and Moore, R.C. (2002). *Pronunciation modelling for improved spelling correction.* Online research report accessed 05 March 2013 at: http://research.microsoft.com/pubs/68884/spell-correct-acl02.pdf

Treiman, R., and Cassar, M. (1997). Spelling acquisition in English. In C.A. Perfetti, L. Rieben, and M. Fayol (Eds.). *Learning to spell: Research, theory, and practice across languages* (pp.61–80). Mahwah, NJ: Erlbaum.

Treiman, R., Stothard, S., and Snowling, M.J. (2013). Instruction matters: Spelling of vowels by children in England and the US. *Reading and Writing: An Interdisciplinary Journal, 26, 3*: 473–487.

Upward, C., and Pulcini, V. (1994). Italian spelling, and how it treats English loan words. *Journal of the Simplified Spelling Society, 20, 1*: 19–23.

Vadasy, P.F., and Sanders, E.A. (2013). Two-year follow-up of a code-oriented intervention for lower-skilled first-graders: The influence of language status and word reading skills on third-grade literacy outcomes. *Reading and Writing: An Interdisciplinary Journal, 26, 6*: 821–843.

Vincent, D., and Crumpler, M. (1997). *British Spelling Tests Series*. Windsor, UK: National Foundation for Educational Research.

Vitale, M.R., Medland, M.B., and Kaniuka, T.S. (2010). Implementing *Spelling through Morphographs* with above-average students in Grade 2: Implications for DI of comparisons with demographically similar control students in Grades 2-3-4-5. *Journal of Direct Instruction, 10,* 1: 17–28.

Wanzek, J., Vaughn, S., Wexler, J., Swanson, E.A., Edmunds, M., and Kim, A.H. (2006). A synthesis of spelling and reading interventions and their effects on the spelling outcomes of students with LD. *Journal of Learning Disabilities, 39,* 6: 528–543.

Washburn, E.K., Joshi, R.M., and Cantrell, E.B. (2011). Are pre-service teachers prepared to teach struggling readers? *Annals of Dyslexia, 61,* 1: 21–43.

Wasowicz, J. (2007). *What do spelling errors tell us about language knowledge?* Online article available on the Learning by Design website, accessed 25 March 2013 at: http://www.learningbydesign.com/uploads/What_Do_Spelling_Errors_Tell_Us_Language_Knowledge.pdf

——(2010). *Improving written language using a multiple-linguistic spelling word study approach*. Online article available on the Learning by Design website, accessed 30 March 2013 at: http://www.learningbydesign.com/uploads/Multiple-Linguistic_Spelling_Word_Study_Approach.pdf

Watson, S. (2013). *The do's and don'ts of spelling lists*. Online item on the About.com website, accessed 21 February 2013 at: http://specialed.about.com/od/literacy/a/spell.htm

Webber, L.A. (2009). *The effect of cognitive imagery training on spelling performance with students with spelling skills deficits*. ProQuest LLC, Ph.D. Dissertation, University of Kansas. ERIC online document ED535580.

Weiser, B., and Mathes, P. (2011). Using encoding instruction to improve the reading and spelling performance of elementary students at risk for literacy difficulties: A best-evidence synthesis. *Review of Educational Research, 81,* 2: 170–200.

Wendon, L. (2006). *Letterland*. Barton, Cambridge, UK: Letterland International.

Werfel, K.L., and Schuele, C.M. (2012). Segmentation and representation of consonant blends in kindergarten children's spellings. *Language, Speech, and Hearing Services in Schools, 43,* 3: 292–307.

Westwood, P. (1999). The correlation between results from different types of spelling test and children's spelling ability while writing. *Australian Journal of Learning Disabilities, 4,* 1: 31–36.

——(2005). *Spelling: Approaches to teaching and assessment* (2nd ed.). Melbourne: Australian Council for Educational Research.

——(2006). *Teaching and learning difficulties*. Melbourne: Australian Council for Educational Research.

——(2011). *Commonsense methods for children with special educational needs* (6th ed.). London: Routledge.

White, S. (2012). *Spelling rules: Syllables, suffixes and vowel sounds*. Online document accessed 24 February 2013 at: http://suite101.com/article/spelling-rules---syllables-suffixes-and-vowel-sounds-a408603

Wigglesworth, G., Simpson, J., and Loakes, D. (2011). NAPLAN language assessments for indigenous children in remote communities: Issues and problems. *Australian Review of Applied Linguistics, 34,* 3: 320–343.

Wilde, S. (2007). *Spelling patterns and strategies.* Portsmouth, NH: Heinemann.

Willet, L., and Gardiner, A. (2009). *Testing spelling: Exploring NAPLAN.* Australian Literacy Educators' Association Conference, 9–12 July 2009. Online document published by the Queensland Studies Authority, accessed 30 March 2013 at: http://www.englishliteracyconference.com.au/files/documents/hobart/conferencePapers/nonRefereed/Willet-Gardiner.pdf

Wood, C., Jackson, E., Hart, L., Plester, B., and Wilde, L. (2011). The effect of text messaging on 9- and 10-year-old children's reading, spelling and phonological processing skills. *Journal of Computer Assisted Learning, 27,* 1: 28–36.

Wu, J., and Zhang, Y. (2010). Examining potentialities of handheld technology in students' academic attainments. *Educational Media International, 47,* 1: 57–67.

Yeung, S.S., Siegel, L., and Chan, C.K.K. (2013). Effects of a phonological awareness program on English reading and spelling among Hong Kong Chinese ESL children. *Reading and Writing: An Interdisciplinary Journal, 26,* 5: 681–704.

Zutell, J. (1979). Spelling strategies of primary school children and their relationship to Piaget's concept of decentration. *Research in English, 13,* 1: 69–80.

——(1996). The Directed Spelling Thinking Activity (DSTA): Providing an effective balance in word study instruction. *The Reading Teacher, 50,* 2: 98–108.

——(1998). Word Sorting: A developmental approach to word study for delayed readers. *Reading and Writing Quarterly, 14*: 219–238.

Index

Main entries are in bold